Efficacy of Visual-Auditory Shadowing Method in SLA
Based on Language Processing
Models in Cognitive Psychology

Efficacy of Visual-Auditory Shadowing Method in SLA Based on Language Processing Models in Cognitive Psychology

NAKAYAMA, Tomokazu

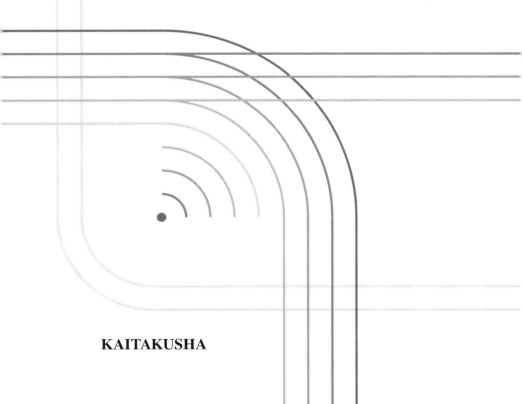

KAITAKUSHA

Kaitakusha Co., Ltd.
5–2, Mukogaoka 1-chome,
Bunkyo-ku, Tokyo 113–0023
Japan

*Efficacy of Visual-Auditory Shadowing Method
in SLA Based on Language Processing Models
in Cognitive Psychology*
by Tomokazu Nakayama

Published in Japan
by Kaitakusha Co., Ltd., Tokyo

Copyright © 2017 by Tomokazu Nakayama

All rights reserved. No part of this publication may be reproduced, stored in a retrieval system, or transmitted, in any form or by any means, electronic, mechanical, photocopying, recording, or otherwise, without the prior permission of the copyright owner.

First published 2017
Second published 2017

Printed and bound in Japan
by Hinode Printing Co., Ltd.

Cover design by Shihoko Nakamura

Preface

Improving listening comprehension in an EFL (English as a Foreign Language) context is quite difficult for two reasons. First, it is because there are much fewer opportunities for EFL learners to listen to the target language outside the classroom, compared to those in an ESL (English as a Second Language) context. The second reason is the phonological differences between the learners' first language and English. Even though it has long been said that there is a need to develop an effective and applicable methodology or instruction to improve listening skills in the EFL context, especially in Japan, it remains to be seen. Therefore, this book tries to develop a new listening methodology for English learners, especially Japanese, who are struggling with improving their listening comprehension. The new methodology is named *visual-auditory shadowing*, which is developed by blending past research findings of the shadowing method and cognitive psychology perspectives. This book attempts to verify this new method. I hope this book can contribute to the improvement of listening skills of EFL learners, especially those of Japanese learners.

Table of Contents

Preface v
Tables x
Figures x
Acknowledgement xi
Note xi

Chapter 1
Issues in L2 Listening Comprehension 1

Introduction 1
Commonalities and Differences in Language Processing 2
Differences between L1 and L2 in Language Processing 5
Priming Effect in Word Recognition 6
The Role of Expectancy in Word Recognition 6
Affecting Factors of Word Recognition in L2 Listening 7
Summary 9

Chapter 2
History on L2 Listening Instruction 11

Listening Through Activation of Bottom-up Processing 11
Listening Through Top-down Processing 12
Post Method Era 13
New Methodologies Based on Past Research 14

Chapter 3

Shadowing as Listening Instruction: Current Perspectives and Research Questions ... 17

Overview of Shadowing ... 17
Activities included in Shadowing Training ... 18
Empirical Studies on Shadowing Training ... 19
Mechanisms of the Shadowing Method ... 20
Self-monitoring during Shadowing Tasks ... 23
Unsolved Issues and Research Questions ... 26

Chapter 4

Theoretical Frameworks Applied in This Research ... 29

Measurement of Listening Comprehension: Situation Model (RQ 1) ... 30
Processing of Language (RQ 1&2) ... 31
Priming Effect (RQ2) ... 38
Purpose of This Research ... 44

Chapter 5

A Study on the Efficacy of Shadowing Training (Study 1) ... 45

Introduction ... 45
Objective ... 45
Method ... 46
Results and Discussion ... 54

Chapter 6

New Shadowing Training Procedures to Facilitate Overall Understanding of Spoken Texts Based on the Findings of Priming Methods ... 57

Introduction ... 57

Effectiveness of Modified Auditory Input for Shadowing (Study 2) 58
    Objective 58
    Method 58
    Results and Discussion 62
Effectiveness of Combination of Reading Aloud and Shadowing (Study 3) 65
    Objective 65
    Method 66
    Results and Discussion 71
Comparison of Shadowing Performance with Different Primes (Study 4) .. 73
    Objective 73
    Method 73
    Results and Discussion 75
Summary 77

Chapter 7
Efficacy of Visual-auditory Shadowing for Listening Comprehension (Study 5) 79

    Introduction 79
    Method 80
    Results and Discussion 84

Chapter 8
Conclusion 89

    Summary 89
    Implications for Pedagogy 92
    Future Research 93

References 95

Index 105

Tables

Table 1 Instruction Procedures in Past Shadowing Method Research *19*
Table 2 Examples of a Passage and Related Questions *48*
Table 3 Lesson Procedures *51*
Table 4 TOEIC Practice Test Scores and the Results of t Tests *54*
Table 5 Scores of Situation Model Listening Comprehension Test and the Results of t Tests *55*
Table 6 The Proportions of the Numbers of Weak Forms and Speech Speeds of the Three Recordings *60*
Table 7 Pretest, Posttest, and Gain Scores in Word Groups Between Groups . *65*
Table 8 Lesson Procedures *70*
Table 9 Pretest, Posttest, and Gain Scores in Word Groups *71*
Table 10 Lesson Procedures *75*
Table 11 Pretest, Posttest, and Gain Scores in Word Groups Between Groups *75*
Table 12 Lesson Procedures *82*
Table 13 Scores on TOEIC Practice Tests and the Results of t Tests *85*
Table 14 Listening Comprehension Test Scores for the Situation Model and the Results of t Tests *86*

Figures

Figure 1. Example questions assigned to control group *50*
Figure 2. Examples of PowerPoint slides for visual shadowing *68*

Acknowledgement

I would like to express my deepest gratitude to Dr. T. Mori, whose enormous support, insightful comments, and warm encouragement were invaluable to me during the course of my study. I would also like to thank Drs. K. Chujo, S. Fukazawa, N. Oka, and Ms. Cheryl Tan, who gave me invaluable comments and constructive advice. Finally, I would like to offer my thanks and blessings to my family and all of those who supported me in any respect during the completion of this project.

Note

This book is based on my Ph.D. thesis submitted to Hiroshima University in February 2013 and consists of five research articles accepted by several journals. Chapter 1 is based on Nakayama (2011c), Chapter 5 on the article Nakayama, Suzuki, and Matsunuma (2015), Chapter 6 on the three articles Nakayama (2011a, 2011b) and Nakayama and Armstrong (2015), and Chapter 7 on Nakayama and Mori (2012).

Efficacy of Visual-Auditory Shadowing Method in SLA Based on Language Processing Models in Cognitive Psychology

Chapter 1

Issues in L2 Listening Comprehension

Introduction

We listen to the news, announcements on trains, and lectures, or read newspapers, neon signs, and books every day. Achieving those everyday tasks is so natural that we are usually not aware of how high the cognitive skills are that we must employ to do so. However, if we do all those tasks in a foreign language, things change. Please take a look at the following number.

12,429,389 yen

Let us assume you are on the phone and you need to correctly write down the above number dictated to you in a foreign language. Do you think you would be able to do it in just one trial or do you think you would ask the speaker to repeat the number? One of the most challenging aspects of learning a foreign language is to acquire listening skills. Numbers are one of the examples posing particular difficulties for second language (L2) learners in listening. The reason for this is rather simple: it is due to their lack of phonological knowledge of numbers. Since numbers are used worldwide, we can process those in our first language (L1) if they are displayed visually, without any trouble in understanding them. But the lack of phonological knowledge of numbers in a foreign language is critical when the information is given in auditory form. If we see it from a different angle, applying knowledge of L1 (knowledge of numbers) to L2 learning can improve learners' listening skills.The question, then, arises of how we can facilitate listening skills by applying reading skills. Past findings in cognitive science indicate commonalities between the reading and listening comprehension process. In other words, applying the strategies or knowledge utilized in the reading process to the listening process can lead to an improvement of listening skills. The focus of this chapter is, first, to discuss the similarities and differences between the reading and listening comprehension process, and then to look for the cause of difficulty in L2 listening comprehension.

Commonalities and Differences in Language Processing

Languages are crucial to both acquiring and conveying information, which is one of the main streams of research in psychology. Research in cognitive science has investigated this matter under the premise that the individual is an active processor of linguistic input.

Influenced by findings in cognitive science, comprehension has become a major concern in the field of second language (L2) acquisition. Although current theories in L2 studies differ in their specifics, most agree with the presumption that three different processes occur in comprehension: encoding, retention, and retrieval (e.g., Atkinson & Shiffrin, 1972; Craik & Lockhart, 1972; Long, 1989; Murdock, 1967). Moreover, the strategies used in listening and reading comprehension procedures are assumed to be similar to each other (Tsui & Fullilove, 1998). In both listening and reading comprehension procedures, listeners/readers need to apply prior knowledge in order to interpret the presented text/talk and predict what they will read/hear, respectively; this strategy is called top-down processing (Goodman, 1967). At the same time, listeners have to decode input accurately to confirm whether their predictions match actual input; this is called bottom-up processing (Carrell, 1983).

Working memory plays a crucial role in language comprehension and refers to a temporary storage buffer with limited capacity; it is responsible for the manipulation of information during the performance of a wide range of everyday tasks, such as language comprehension (Baddeley, 1986; Baddeley & Logie, 1999). Languages are primarily expressed in two modalities: verbal (auditory) and written (visual). Recent research has indicated common points between the processing of verbal and visual linguistic information in working memory (Baddeley, 1986, 2000; Baddeley, Lewis, & Vallar, 1984; Baddeley, Thomson, & Buchanan, 1975; Logie, 1995). Other studies have also indicated that how we process information in working memory affects the duration of its retention (Atkinson & Shiffrin, 1971; Craik & Lockhart, 1972; Hyde & Jenkins, 1969; Miller, 1956; Murdock, 1967; Parkin, 1984; Santrock, 1988). Furthermore, the understanding of both written and spoken text can be expressed in three different types of mental representations: surface structure, propositional textbase, and the situation model (Kintsch, 1994; Kintsch, Welsch, Schmalhofer, & Zimny, 1990).

Past research findings therefore indicate the following three similarities between reading and listening comprehension procedures: 1) the strategies utilized in comprehension procedures in both listening and reading conditions are similar (see Chapter 2); 2) both verbal and visual linguistic information go through the same process in working memory (see Chapter3); and 3) the comprehension of both written and spoken text can be expressed in three different types of mental representations (see Chapter 4).

Even though reading and listening comprehension have procedures in common, there is a critical difference between them. According to Kadota (2007), it is how we process the input, because of the differences in modality. In reading, we process written input. Readers are hence able to control the time it takes for them to do so. If they miss some words, they can go back and read them again. This is referred to as "off-line" processing. On the other hand, in listening, listeners cannot control the time of processing the input since the sounds of the words will disappear as soon as they have been uttered, while the speed of utterances further differs from speaker to speaker. It is impossible for listeners to go back to missed words unless they have the chance to ask speakers to repeat them again. So listening requires "on-line" processing, since listeners are required to process the input in real time.

Differences between L1 and L2 in Language Processing

When the message is conveyed in our native language, we are not usually so concerned with whether it is mediated by auditory or visual input. Many researchers argue that cognitive activities may differ in the amount of attention and effort they require. Some cognitive operations require only minimal effort and become very rapid in the L1, owing to a considerable amount of prior practice and/or exposure, whereas in the L2, they require considerable attention and are relatively slower (Favreau & Segalowitz, 1983). The former is characterized as automatic and the latter as controlled (Shiffrin & Schneider, 1977; Shiffrin, Dumais, & Schneider, 1981).

The complex activity of listening involves a number of highly practiced operations that are likely to be fairly automatic in the L1 (Favreau & Segalowitz, 1983). However, in the L2, these processes often require conscious effort (Favreau & Segalowitz, 1983). For many L2 learners, certain cognitive operations underlying reading may be automatic, but the same operations may not be automatic in the domain of listening (Field, 2003; Nakayama & Iwata, 2012). For example, even L2 listeners with an intermediate level of skill often mistake auditory input such as "I won't leave the room" as "I want to leave the room," although they can understand the same input if it is presented textually (Nakayama & Iwata, 2012). Thus, one way to look for such differences between reading and listening in the L2 is at the level of word recognition.

Priming Effect in Word Recognition

Current research findings using priming methods (Neely, 1977; Posner & Snyder, 1975; Tweedy, Lapinsky, & Schvaneveldt, 1977) address the differences in role between automatic and controlled processing in word recognition. Language users tend to process a word more quickly and/or accurately when they have been previously exposed to another word that is related in meaning. For example, the word BREAD will be responded to faster if the word BUTTER has recently been seen or heard. This phenomenon is called the semantic priming effect: it suggests that semantically related words (like BREAD and BUTTER) are stored together or somehow linked in the mind (Meyer & Schvaneveldt, 1971). Both automatic and controlled forms of processing are responsible for this phenomenon (Favreau & Segalowitz, 1983). Controlled processing is partly responsible, because subjects' expectancies can influence the magnitude of the semantic priming effect (Favreau & Segalowitz, 1983; Neely, 1977). Automatic processing also has a role, because the priming effect can be observed under conditions in which subjects have little expectancy to observe a semantically associated prime-target word pair (Favreau & Segalowitz, 1983).

The Role of Expectancy in Word Recognition

Neely (1977) provided significant evidence that subjects' expectancies greatly influence the magnitude of the priming effect. He used lexical decision tasks in which subjects were asked to decide whether a target string of letters was a word or a non-word. Subjects were told the patterns of prime-target combinations. For example, they were told that if the prime was BIRD, most often the following words would be the names of birds. They were also told that if the prime was BODY or BUILDING, the following words would usually be parts of bodies or buildings, respectively. However, the subjects were then asked to process unexpected targets. Those unexpected words were categorized as the following two types: unexpected targets that were semantically unrelated to the prime (BIRD-DOOR) and those that were semantically related to the prime (BODY-HEAD). Neely (1977) found that responses to the expected targets were faster in both cases; however, responses to the unexpected targets declined in comparison with the control condition. To summarize, in addition to the automatic process of word recognition in semantic memory, subjects' expectancies with respect to the input greatly influence the speed and/or accuracy of word recognition. In other words, the better the subjects' expectancies conform to the input, the better or more rapid the processing of the input that takes place.

Factors Affecting Word Recognition in L2 Listening

What kinds of factors related to L2 learners' expectancies are, then, considered to affect word recognition in L2 listening? One factor is the difference between the rhythmic structures of the native and target languages (Koike, 1993; Sudo, 2010). Japanese is a "mora-timed rhythm language," in which each mora takes the same amount of time to be pronounced. If the number of morae contained in an utterance is larger, it takes more time for them to be produced. On the other hand, English is "a stress-timed rhythm language," in which stressed syllables occur at about the same intervals; the time taken to produce an utterance scales with the number of stressed syllables it contains. Therefore, even an utterance with a large number of syllables takes approximately the same amount of time to be produced as an utterance containing the same number of stressed syllables but fewer syllables overall.

Because of these differences in rhythmic structures between Japanese and English, spoken English is different from what Japanese L2 learners would expect on the basis of visual information. English auditory input has unique features, such as connected speech, reduced forms, weak verbs, assimilation, elision, resyllabification, and cliticization—none of which exist in Japanese. In English, a single word can even have different sound qualities depending on where it is placed in a phrase or sentence. L2 listeners with limited knowledge of English or weak listening skills are often confused by these phonetic variations, resulting in misunderstandings, even though they may be able to grasp the meaning if the same words are presented as visual input (Field, 2003).

The other factor that affects word recognition in L2 listening is the frequency with which L2 learners are exposed to spoken English outside of the classroom (Field, 2003). The amount of time spent listening to English by L2 learners in Japan is limited by comparison with ESL (English as a second language) learners, namely, those who learn English in English-speaking countries. In Japan, the major language in use outside of the classroom is Japanese. Therefore, L2 learners only have contact with spoken English output in classrooms, unless they create opportunities to listen to English on their own. Furthermore, according to Tamai (2005), the time allotted to listening activities inside and outside of English L2 classes in Japan is considerably limited compared with that dedicated to reading activities.

Therefore, many researchers claim that the acquisition of listening comprehension skills requires more time and effort than that of reading comprehension. Many previous studies have suggested that some reading comprehension skills of proficient L2 learners can be applied to listening in spite of the learners' lack of contact with spoken output outside of their classrooms (e.g., Call, 1985; Chamot & Kupper, & O'Malley, 1989; Field, 2003; Favreau & Segalowitz, 1983, 1999; Kadota, 2007; Koike, 1993; Richards, 1983; Sudo, 2010).

Summary

This chapter has provided an overview of language processing and addressed issues in L2 listening comprehension. Even though both reading and listening comprehension share similar strategies and processing in working memory, there is a critical difference between them. Reading is an off-line process whereby readers can control the time taken to process the input, while listening is on-line process since listeners cannot control the time they have to process the input. Moreover, acquiring listening comprehension skills in the L2 requires more time and effort than the acquisition of reading comprehension skills. The main reason for this is differences in word recognition processes. Since pronunciation varies from person to person, learners need to expend their attentional resources on decoding the speaker's utterances. And the frequency with which L2 learners are exposed to spoken English outside of the classroom is limited. Especially, in the case of English as a foreign language (EFL), learners have contact with spoken English output only in classrooms unless they create opportunities to listen to the language on their own. To improve listening skills, many researchers suggest that the reading comprehension skills of proficient L2 learners can be applied to listening comprehension skills. In other words, if we can find an efficient way to apply reading comprehension skills to listening, then listening skills can be improved at least to the level equivalent to reading skills. How, then, can we improve listening skills in the L2 so that they match the level of reading skills? In the next chapter, I will conduct a brief historical overview of previous research on L2 listening instruction to identify some preliminary answers.

Chapter 2

History of L2 Listening Instruction

"Listen and Repeat": Influence of Behaviorism in Second Language Acquisition

The first approach to listening instruction is said to have been the "listen and repeat" (audio-lingual) approach, which emerged in the 1940s (Vandergrift, 2004) and was further developed into the 1950s. It was based on theories in behaviorism and structural linguistics. Behaviorism claims that psychology should limit its concerns to the observable behaviors of humans or animals, and one of its premises is that acquisition takes place by linking a new behavior to a stimulus through reinforcement. In short, under behaviorism, the individual is regarded as a passive recipient of information.

At the same time, the United States became the center of research on structural linguistics. Fries (1945) and Lado (1950) proposed a contrastive analysis hypothesis, which claims that L2 learning is facilitated by knowledge of the intricate details of both L1 and L2.

In classrooms applying the audio-lingual approach, which was strongly influenced by theories in behaviorism and structural linguistics, listening instruction was perceived as a passive activity. In those classrooms, acquisition took place through endless repetitions of "listen and repeat." However, many researchers claimed that knowledge acquired through the audio-lingual method was not applicable to more complex interactive activities such as daily communication (Richards & Rodgers, 2001).

Listening Through Top-down Processing: Schema Theory

The field of cognitive psychology emerged in the middle of the 1950s. It investigates humans' mental abilities, such as perceiving, learning, remembering, thinking, reasoning, and understanding, by applying information processing models. Unlike behaviorism, cognitive psychology sees a human being as an active information processor with a mind capable of solving problems. Perspectives and theories developed in the field of cognitive psychology have strongly influenced psycholinguistics and related fields, such as L2 acquisition.

Bartlett (1932) studied how people remembered stories and found that they left parts out, added information not mentioned in the original stories, and even reconstructed the plots to match their own contexts. This idea was formalized as schema theory, which asserts the importance of individual background knowledge on the formation of textual understanding (Bartlett, 1932; Rumelhart, 1980; Rumelhart & Ortony, 1977). According to this theory, a visual or verbal text can only specify which information the reader/listener should retrieve or match with background knowledge for the purpose of textual comprehension. According to Rumelhart (1980), the comprehension of visually or verbally presented input simultaneously requires both linguistic knowledge of the input and access to one's background knowledge. Schema theory has had considerable impact on studies of L2 listening and its instruction (e.g., Goodman, 1967; Asher, 1972; Herron, York, Cole, & Linden, 1998; Ginther, 2002; Jones & Plass, 2002; Markham, Peter, & McCarthy, 2001). However, excessive dependence on a schema causes communication breakdown if it is not appropriate to the context (Lynch, 1998; Mendelsohn, 1998; Oxford, 1993; Rost, 2002; Rubin, 1994; Vandergrift, 2004).

Post Method Era

Along with the development of studies in cognitive psychology in the 1980s, the mechanism of L2 listening processes and the factors that affect and facilitate L2 listening were elucidated and hierarchized as some of the highest cognitive activities. One major finding is that both the facilitation of top-down processing by activation of schema and bottom-up processing—which requires detailed processing of phonemes into words, phrases, and sentences—are necessary to facilitate L2 listening. This is called the Interactive Activation Model, which is claimed by Rumelhart, Hinton, and Williams (1986) to draw upon parallel distributed processing. Many researchers of L2 listening instruction have conducted empirical research to confirm the significance of the mechanism behind the Interactive Activation Model (Hirai, 1999; Lynch, 1998; Mendelsohn, 1998; O'Malley, Chamot, & Kupper,

1989; Tsui & Fullilove, 1998). These researchers cite the differences between bottom-up and top-down processing and argue for the necessity of a new method or approach to facilitate bottom-up processing while listening. On the basis of previous findings on bottom-up and top-down processing, Brown (2006) describes 14 basic skills that are necessary for L2 learners to exercise as they acquire effective listening comprehension skills.

However, the field of L2 studies in the 1980s has often been called "the post method era," during which research focused on cognitive processing by learners rather than on the development of methods or approaches to facilitate L2 listening. Therefore, though the significance of skills in facilitating listening has been pointed out by many researchers, few actual methods to improve bottom-up processing for listening have been developed (e.g., O'Malley, Chamot, & Kupper, 1989; Richards, 1983; Rubin, 1994).

New Methodologies Based on Past Research

In the late 1990s, research in the field of cognitive science on the cognitive processing involved in listening and reading comprehension began to focus on empirical research on the L2 listening instruction methods that were already being practiced in Japan. For example, though dictation was a popular method of listening instruction in practice, very little empirical research had been conducted on its effectiveness in actually improving L2 listening comprehension. In dictation, students are asked to write exactly what they hear; generally, it has been thought to be effective for the improvement of not only listening copmprehension but also compostion, vocabulary building, and grammatical skills (Shirahata, Wakabayashi, & Muranoi, 2010). However, empirical studies (Oyama, 2009; Tamai, 1992; Yanagihara, 1995) have not shown clear evidence of the effectiveness of dictation.

Furthermore, empirical studies on listening instruction methods that were mainly practiced in professional translator training began to receive the attention of SLA researchers in the 1990s. For example, though sight-translation had been widely applied in translation courses, it had received little attention from researchers in cognitive science until the 1990s. In sight-translation, learners are asked to visually chunk information presented in a foreign language and translate those chunks into their native langue by vocalizing their meanings. Lambert (2004) argues that sight-translation is effective at improving listening comprehension skills. On the other hand, Takizawa (2002) maintains that sight-translation is so intense, requiring so much attention and training, that it is not suitable for most pedagogical situations. Findings on the effectiveness of sight translation differ among researchers; recently, "shadowing" has become a topic of focus, the existing literature on which will be discussed in the next chapter.

Chapter 3

Shadowing as Listening Instruction: Current Perspectives and Research Questions

Overview of Shadowing

Empirical research on the shadowing method began in the 1990s. According to Tamai (2005), shadowing refers to "listening in which the learners track what [they] heard in speech and repeat it as accurately as possible while listening attentively to the incoming information" (p. 34). Shadowing gained attention as a method to investigate the processing of auditory perception and selective attention (Lambert, 1988; Yanagihara, 1995). The use of shadowing for listening instruction in translator training, which is a combination of shadowing and other activities such as the reading aloud of a script became popular in the 1970s (Tamai, 2005). The implementation of the shadowing method in translator training captured the attention of L2 learning researchers in the 1990s—especially in Japan—and the effectiveness of the shadowing method in L2 settings became the object of empirical investigation.

Activities Included in Shadowing Training

As stated above, the shadowing method is a set of listening instructions including shadowing and other activities, such as reading aloud. Although some empirical studies have shown the effectiveness of the shadowing method in L2 settings, instruction procedures differ among researchers, as shown in Table 1.

All of the researchers whose studies are listed in Table 1 chose a listening activity as the first task. Kadota (2007) argues that learners need to grasp the overall meaning of a text before they engage in shadowing activities. Moreover, the second task, called "mumbling" was also a listening activity. It served as a warm-up for the next activity of "prosody shadowing." Mumbling asks learners to shadow the auditory input without saying it clearly; this is considered to help learners ready themselves for prosody shadowing, which asks learners to repeat the input aloud (Kadota, 2007). In addition to shadowing, some activities with visual information, such as parallel reading (which asks learners to read the transcript aloud along with the auditory input), reading aloud, or silent reading, are conducted in the shadowing method. After the third task described in Table 1, a reading comprehension exercise was conducted in all investigated studies with the exception of the one by Tamai (2005).

Every study in Table 1 adopted a combination of shadowing tasks and some activity related to reading aloud. Although the shadowing method is considered to combine shadowing with reading aloud, little research has been conducted on how the activities of shadowing and reading aloud interact to generate improvement in learners' listening comprehension. One possible reason for this lack of investigation is that researchers have followed the assumption of its effectiveness that has been cultivated in the education of translators.

Table 1

Instruction Procedures in Past Shadowing Method Research

Procedure	Tamai (1992, 1997, 2005)	Yanagihara (1995)	Karasawa (2009)	Kadota (2007)	Iwashita (2008)
1	Listening	Listening	Listening	Listening	Listening
2	*Reading aloud	Reading comprehension	Reading aloud	Mumbling	Silent reading
3	Vocabulary check	*Reading aloud	Shadowing	*Reading aloud	*Reading aloud
4	Shadowing	Shadowing	Reading comprehension	Reading comprehension	Shadowing
5			**Shadowing	Shadowing	
6			Reading aloud	**Shadowing	
7			Shadowing	Repeating	

Note. *Kadota (2007) also calls this "parallel reading." **This is also called "content shadowing," whereby learners are asked to comprehend the input and shadow at the same time.

Empirical Studies on Shadowing Training

Many previous studies have investigated the efficacy of shadowing for the improvement of listening comprehension in L2 settings (Sakoda, Furumoto, Nakagami, Sakamoto, & Goto, 2009; Sato & Nakamura, 1998; Tamai, 1992; Yanagihara, 1995). For example, Tamai (1992) and Yanagihara (1995) compared the shadowing method with dictation, reporting the former to lead to greater improvement in listening.

Moreover, research has also investigated how much time is required for the shadowing method to produce improvement in listening. Tamai (1997) reported the efficacy of 90-min shadowing training sessions for 5 consecutive days in improving the listening of university students, accordingly arguing that even short-term intensive training is effective.

Previous findings indicate that the shadowing method can produce greater improvements in listening than dictation. However, the number of previous studies on the topic is limited, and little research has been conducted on the effectiveness of the shadowing method for various aspects of listening comprehension compared with the listening instruction widely used in current pedagogical settings in Japan.

Mechanisms of the Shadowing Method

Researchers have also tried to investigate why the shadowing method brings about improvement in listening comprehension. Many researchers in cognitive science agree that working memory plays a significant role in language comprehension (e.g., Baddeley, Gathercole, & Papagno, 1998; Papagno, Valentine, & Baddeley, 1991). Among various processes conducted in working memory, phonological coding is considered to play a significant role in language comprehension. Phonological coding is the process of converting the incoming linguistic input (visual or auditory input) into the recipient's own voice (Baddeley, 1986).

Attention and Working Memory in Language Comprehension

Cognitive activities require different degrees of attention (Baddeley, 1986; LaBerge & Samuels, 1974; Posner & Snyder, 1975; Shiffrin & Schneider, 1977). Some of them require minimal attention and occur relatively rapidly, whereas others require considerable attention and occur very slowly. The complex activity of listening requires multiple cognitive processes to occur at once, such as phonemic and lexical analysis, syntactic and semantic analysis, and the interpretation of the processed utterance. Since attentional resources are limited, a high demand for processes that consume too much attention often results in the breakdown of comprehension (Baddeley, 1986; Kadota, 2007; Tamai, 2005).

Working memory plays a crucial role in language comprehension, whereby it performs three functions: phonological coding, retention for later retrieval, and processing (Baddeley, 1986; Baddeley & Logie, 1999). Phonological coding is the process of internal vocalization of orthographical information (visual input) or phonological information (auditory input) for retention, later retrieval, and processing for comprehension (Atkinson & Shiffrin, 1971; Baddeley, 1986, 2000). Since the capacity of working memory is limited, a high demand for phonological coding results in the slowdown of computation, which causes information to be inaccessible for later comprehension processing (Baddeley, 1986, 2000; Tamai, 2005). In L2 listeners, phonetic variations in auditory input often slow the speed of phonological coding, resulting in the partial or total loss of information needed for comprehension (Kadota, 2007; Nakayama et al. 2015; Tamai, 2005). In other words, facilitating the learning of phonetic variations in auditory input might lead to improvement in the phonological coding of auditory input, which could free attentional resources for the higher cognitive processes necessary for comprehension.

Tamai (2005) and Kurata (2007) conducted research on whether the shadowing method brings about improvements in phonological coding. Hypothesizing shadowing to be a vocalized version of phonological coding, Tamai (2005) investigated whether phonological coding processes could be improved by the shadowing method. The study's findings suggest that phonological coding improves with training. Tamai (2005) concluded that the shadowing method improves the phonological coding process in a way that facilitates higher and more complex processing for comprehension.

The phonological coding process is considered to occur in a phonological loop (Baddeley, 1986). Kurata (2007) investigated the relationship between the capacity of the phonological loop and shadowing performance, with the results suggesting that larger phonological loop capacity yields better shadowing performance. Both Tamai (2005) and Kurata (2007) concluded that the shadowing method of listening instruction facilitates listening comprehension skills by training learners' phonological coding processes.

Validity of the Shadowing Method

Researchers have also investigated at which levels of proficiency the shadowing method is most effective. Sato and Nakamura (1998),

Tamai (2005), and Yanagihara (1995) employed the shadowing method on university students with advanced, intermediate, and lower intermediate levels of listening comprehension skills, comparing the improvement of the three groups. Significant improvement was observed only in the intermediate and lower intermediate students.

Self-monitoring during Shadowing Tasks

Although previous findings suggest that the shadowing method is especially effective for learners of intermediate and lower intermediate level, Ochi (2005) and Tanaka (2004) have argued that this method is too cognitively demanding for the lower intermediate (as well as novice) students. Ochi (2005) and Tanaka (2004) applied the shadowing method to Japanese high school and university students with no prior knowledge of it. The results of questionnaires administered at the end of training suggest that shadowing, which trains listening and speaking at the same time, requires so much of the learners' attention that they cannot self-monitor to check their performance while they shadow.

The fact that shadowing consumes considerable attention has also been indicated by other studies. For example, Gerver (1974) and Lambert (1988) investigated which of three conditions (listening, simultaneous translation, and shadowing) facilitated the memory of speech content among professional French translators whose first language was English. The findings of both studies suggest that shadowing facilitated recall the least of the three conditions. Therefore, shadowing is such a complex cognitive activity that even professional translators who are considered to be skilled in shadowing fail to completely remember the content of speech when they engage in shadowing.

L1 shadowing research (Carey, 1971; Kurata, 2008) has reported almost the same results as Gerver (1974) and Lambert (1988). Carey (1971) compared the listening condition to the shadowing condition, finding that the recall of speech content differs according to the speed of auditory input. Carey (1971) suggests that if a shadower can adjust his/her voice to the auditory input, recall of speech content is facilitated more than in the listening condition. Iwashita (2008) and Kurata (2008) investigated whether shadowing facilitates not only auditory perception but also semantic processing in native Japanese speakers. However, these researchers proved only that auditory perception processing is improved by shadowing. This result further indicates that shadowing is a complex and cognitively demanding task. Past research findings in native and foreign languages further suggest that shadowing is a cognitively demanding task to be applied in pedagogical settings; therefore, some scaffolding is necessary to facilitate self-monitoring while shadowing.

Learning strategies are "the special thoughts or behaviors that individuals use to help them comprehend, learn, or retain new information" (O'Malley & Chamot, 1990). Learners who cannot use proper learning strategies to achieve their tasks often fail in those tasks. One such learning strategy is the "self-monitoring strategy," in which learners perform on-line monitoring of how well they execute their tasks. The self-monitoring strategy has been defined as a significant factor affecting learning (O'Malley, Chamot, & Kupper, 1989). However, cognitively demanding tasks such as shadowing often divert the attentional resources necessary to engage in self-monitoring. According to Ban (2004), an efficient way to enhance self-monitoring strategy is thus to record learners' performance and have them review the recordings after performing the task. Ban (2004) asked JSL (Japanese as second language) learners to record their voices while they practiced pronunciation and then to listen to the recordings immediately afterwards. Her findings suggested better improvement in pronunciation in the self-monitoring group than the control group.

According to Chamot and Kupper (1989), self-monitoring has two significant roles. One is to recognize mistakes on-line, and the other is to correct those mistakes on-line. Nakayama and Suzuki (2012), following Chamot and Kupper (1989) and Ban (2004), investigated the effectiveness of two methods to supplement self-monitoring. Nakayama and Suzuki (2012) divided 35 university students (male $n = 32$; female $n = 3$) into three groups and compared their shadowing performance. One was the "self-monitoring group," in which participants were asked to underline the words they had successfully shadowed on a transcript, listening to their shadowed voices as soon as they had finished each shadowing trial. Another group was called the "pair-work group," in which learners placed in pairs listened to their partners' shadowed voices, underlining the successfully shadowed words. The learners were also asked to give feedback on their partners' shadowing performances in Japanese after each trial. The other group was a control group, in which learners were asked to shadow and to check their own shadowing performance by looking at the transcript.

Nakayama and Suzuki (2012) compared the participants' shadowing performance by group: learners were asked to shadow words before and after the different types of intervention. They focused on different types of words (function words vs. content words), and not just the total gain score, throughout the experiment. English vocabulary consists of two different word groups: function and content words. Content words are nouns, adjectives, or verbs that have lexical meanings rather than predominantly serving syntactic functions. Function words, such as prepositions, conjunctions, and articles—which mainly indicate syntactic relationships rather than semantic meanings—often change in terms of pronunciation according their placement within sentences (as weak forms of function words), whereas content words do not. Therefore, because of the differences in rhythmic structures between English and Japanese, identifying function words in auditory input is often difficult for Japanese L2 learners (Koike, 1993). More careful observation is necessary for learners to perform shadowing on function words than on content words.

The results of Nakayama and Suzuki (2012) suggested that the self-monitoring group had better shadowing performance. However, it remains unclear whether or not self-monitoring is effective for function words.

Unsolved Issues and Research Questions

Past research has clearly defined the efficacy and mechanisms of shadowing methods. First, the shadowing method combines shadowing and reading aloud and is especially effective for lower intermediate learners. Second, shadowing is deeply related to the phonological coding process in working memory, which in turn is responsible for the temporary retention of incoming information for further processing and for the retrieval of semantic information from long-term memory. Furthermore, previous research has also suggested that shadowing is a complex and highly cognitively demanding task, especially for beginners or lower-level learners. Nakayama and Suzuki (2012) therefore developed an effective method to supplement self-monitoring among such learners.

However, previous findings also indicate two unresolved issues. First, little research has been conducted on how the shadowing method differs in effectiveness from the traditional listening instruction that predominates in current pedagogical settings in Japan. Second, little research has been conducted on how shadowing and reading aloud activities interact in the shadowing method for the improvement of listening comprehension. This research aims to resolve these two issues by answering the following two research questions:

RQ 1: At which level of understanding is the shadowing method especially effective, and if so, how does shadowing differ in effectiveness from the listening instruction mainly practiced in pedagogical settings?

RQ 2: Is a new shadowing method that reinforces the phonological coding process by combining shadowing and reading aloud more effective than the shadowing method currently practiced in pedagogical settings in terms of shadowing performance and comprehension?

This research will investigate these two research questions according to the theoretical frameworks described in the next chapter.

Chapter 4

Theoretical Frameworks Applied in This Research

As described in Chapter 1 through 3, the current state of knowledge in L2 research is a result of gains in understanding made in the realm of cognitive science. The main concern of cognitive psychology is to investigate how L1 languages are processed, and models of current L2 studies originated from L1 studies in the field of cognitive psychology. For example, the L2 listening model of O'Malley et al. (1989), which has been highly cited in L2 research, maintains that L2 listening comprehension consists of three different processes: perception, parsing, and utilization. Actually, this model was first proposed by Anderson (1983), who is a researcher in the field of cognitive psychology. Many L2 models originated from L1 findings in cognitive psychology with modifications that reflect L2 settings (e.g., Richards, 1983; Tamai, 2005; Vandergrift, 2004). However, current L2 models are incapable of addressing the two research questions of this research. Therefore, this research will adopt three additional theoretical frameworks from L1 studies in the field of cognitive psychology.

Measurement of Listening Comprehension: The Situation Model (RQ 1)

Previous findings suggest that there are different levels of listening comprehension. Therefore, to answer RQ 1, we need to know at which levels of textual understanding the shadowing method is especially effective and how it differs in effectiveness from the listening instruction mainly practiced in current pedagogical settings. It is necessary to adopt another theoretical framework to investigate the effectiveness of the shadowing method at various levels of understanding and its contributions to learning transfer. Therefore, this book adopts the model of van Dijk and Kintsch (1983) to investigate at which levels of understanding the shadowing method is effective.

This study applies the situation model of Kintsch et al. (1990) to measure comprehension. To fully understand a text, it is necessary to create a coherent mental representation that is integrated with one's prior knowledge (Bransford & Johnson, 1972; van Dijk & Kintsch, 1983). It is known that three different levels of representations—*surface structure*, *textbase*, and *situation model*—are constructed in the process of mental representation (van Dijk & Kintsch, 1983). The surface structure is a representation of the text itself before any syntactic and semantic processing; the textbase consists of the elements directly described in the text through syntactic and semantic processing thereof; and the situation model is the highest level, corresponding to a situational description constructed on the basis of the text and one's prior knowledge and experiences (McNamara & Kintsch, 1996). Comprehension of a text is considered complete when an appropriate situation model is constructed by the recipient (Kintsch et al., 1990). Although this theoretical framework (van Dijk & Kintsch, 1983) is based on reading comprehension research, it is applicable to the measurement of listening comprehension as well, since reading and listening comprehension have certain processes in common (Baddeley, 1986; Baddeley, Gathercole, & Papagno, 1998).

Processing of Language (RQ 1 & 2)

In answering RQ 1, this research will reveal at which levels of understanding the shadowing method is especially effective and how it differs in effectiveness from the listening instruction methods that predominate in pedagogical settings; to accomplish this, the model of Kintsch et al. (1990) will be applied. If learners do not create the type of situation model described in the study by Kintsch et al. (1990) by current shadowing methods, a new shadowing method will be necessary to facilitate learners' attainment of that stage—a line of reasoning that is related to RQ 2. To investigate the relationship between the processing of visual and auditory input, it is necessary to understand how language is processed. A different theoretical framework is necessary to investigate the relationship between the processing of visual and auditory input. Therefore, the next section will detail how both visual and auditory input are processed and propose another theoretical framework.

Cognitive psychology stipulates that three levels of processing are involved in language processing: encoding, retention, and retrieval. Furthermore, human memory consists of three different memory types: sensory register, working memory, and long-term memory (Mori & Chujo, 2005).

Input is stored in sensory registers for a very short period. Visually presented input is stored in iconic memory, which is one of the sensory registers; auditory input is stored in echoic memory, which is another type of sensory register. Unless attention is given to the information stored in sensory registers, it is lost in a very short period. Iconic memory can maintain visual input for less than 1 s, and echoic memory can store auditory input for about 5 s. Only the information in the sensory registers to which attention is given is encoded and sent to working memory for rehearsal and subsequent storage in and retrieval from long-term memory.

Working memory refers to a temporal buffer of limited capacity that plays a role in the temporal storage of information; it carries out demanding cognitive tasks such as comprehension, learning, and reasoning (Baddeley, 2000; Baddeley & Hitch, 1974; Miller, 1956). Working memory plays an active role in human cognitive activities.

The model of Baddeley (1986, 2000) is often called a multicomponent model. This model assumes that there is one controlling device, called a central executive, and three *slave* systems. One of the slave systems is called the visuospatial sketchpad: it processes visual and spatial images coming from iconic memory that cannot be textualized for attention. Another slave system of the central executive is called the phonological loop, in which auditory input from echoic memory is processed. The phonological loop has a phonological short-term store that uses attention to preserve auditory input coming from echoic memory for a very short time. Baddeley (2000) recently added the third slave system, which is called the episodic buffer. This component is assumed to be a limited-capacity temporary buffer that comes from a variety of sources, including visual, auditory, and tactile input. The episodic buffer accepts many kinds of input, but the other systems only accept certain kinds. This buffer is called episodic because it plays an essential role in sending visual and spatial information into and retrieving information from episodic long-term memory according to commands from the central executive. Episodic long-term memory refers to knowledge of incidents that happened in a certain place at a certain time (Tulving, 1972); it is considered to be part of long-term memory. The role of the central executive is to allocate the limited cognitive resources of working memory to its slave systems and to control the flow of information within the systems of working memory.

One commonality between visual and auditory linguistic information is that both are processed by the phonological loop, whereby they are considered to be subvocalized for subsequent encoding or retention. The dual-task method is usually used to investigate the commonalities between the processing of visual and auditory linguistic information (e.g., Baddeley et al., 1975; Baddeley et al., 1984). In the dual-task method, subjects are asked to perform two tasks: the primary and the secondary task. The cognitive resources of working memory are limited, so that when two tasks are executed simultaneously, they share the same cognitive resources. When insufficient cognitive resources to perform both the primary and secondary tasks are available, performance of both tasks is affected (Baddeley, 1986). By comparing the outcome of two simultaneous tasks with those of the single tasks, we can evaluate how resources are shared between the tasks. Articulatory suppression is usually used as a secondary task when investigating the roles of the phonological loop; in this task, the participants repeat nonwords or count numbers (e.g., one, two, three, four, five) verbally while engaging in the primary task (e.g., memorization of a list of words). The secondary task is considered to prevent the participants from rehearsing the words to be remembered in the phonological loop.

Individuals find it harder to accurately recall phonologically similar words (e.g., bat, pat, mat) than dissimilar words (e.g., pen, hug, dip), regardless of whether the words are presented verbally or visually (Baddeley, 1986; Conrad & Hull, 1964). This phenomenon is called the phonological similarity effect. It has also been investigated using the dual-task method: while participants memorize a list of phonologically similar words as the primary task, they are asked to verbally repeat the numbers from 1 to 10 sequentially as the secondary task. By repeating the numbers sequentially, the participants' encoding of the visually presented words in the phonological loop is affected, leading to the disappearance of the phonological similarity effect. However, if the dual task employs auditory input, the effect does not disappear. This finding provides evidence that not only verbal but also visual linguistic information is phonologically encoded in the phonological loop.

People usually recall sequences of short words (e.g., stop, sun, drug) more easily than sequences of long words (e.g., unfriendly, university, alternatively), because long words take more time than short ones to be encoded in the phonological loop. The capacity of the phonological loop is limited, and the more time required for rehearsal, the less information it can hold. The word-length effect will disappear if articulatory suppression is conducted while materials are presented both visually and verbally (Baddeley et al., 1975; Baddeley et al., 1984).

Logie (1995) describes both visual and verbal linguistic information as being encoded in the phonological loop, whereby it is internally vocalized for retention or retrieval of information from long-term memory. This process is common to visual and verbal linguistic information.

As described in Chapter 3, Tamai (2005) argues that the shadowing method improves listening comprehension by promoting the phonological coding process of auditory input. However, activities related to the processing of visual input, such as reading aloud, are included in the training procedures of the shadowing method. Moreover, little research has been conducted on how such activities influence shadowing performance.

According to Brown (2006), there are two ways to read text to facilitate the comprehension of visual input in second or foreign languages: silent reading and reading aloud. Silent reading has three subcategories: *intensive reading*, *skimming*, and *rapid reading*. In intensive reading, learners are asked to read every word carefully, considering its meaning and syntactic structure. In skimming, readers are required to grasp key words—such as the topic of the text—to glean the main ideas from the text. In rapid reading, readers are asked to read the text as quickly as possible to grasp its overall meaning, usually without re-reading. As described in Table 1, Iwashita (2008) applied silent reading to shadowing methods.

As for the relationship between silent reading and listening comprehension in an L2, Oyama (2009) investigated the effectiveness of rapid reading training, which is claimed to facilitate the on-line processing of visual text for listening comprehension. Oyama (2009) split participants into rapid reading and dictation groups and gave weekly 10-min training sessions for 8 consecutive weeks. Analysis of the pre- and posttests revealed that the rapid reading group outperformed the dictation group. On the basis of this result, Oyama (2009) concluded that rapid reading training improves listening comprehension skills.

However, the facilitation of on-line processing by rapid reading training does not resolve the issue of the comprehension gap between visual input and auditory input observed by Nakayama and Iwata (2012). The study by Nakayama and Iwata (2012) showed that visual input yielded better comprehension than auditory input. However, the assertion by Oyama (2009) that the comprehension of visual input is facilitated by rapid reading training—leading to better performance in listening comprehension—fails to address the issue raised by Nakayama and Iwata (2012).

According to Baddeley (1986), phonological coding of visual input only takes place for complex messages. In other words, simple text is directly processed for comprehension from visual input without any phonological coding. Therefore, under silent-reading conditions, it is possible for learners to comprehend text even if they cannot pronounce the words precisely. However, under listening conditions, it is impossible to understand text without precise phonetic knowledge of the words. Therefore, even simple text can cause comprehension gaps depending on the modality in which the text is presented.

In sum, the facilitation of on-line processing of visual input by rapid reading proposed by Oyama (2009) might also facilitate the processing of auditory input. However, the assertion of Oyama (2009)

Chapter 4 Theoretical Frameworks Applied in This Research

differs from that of this book.

This research will adopt the type of reading aloud activity applied in the studies by Kadota (2007), Karasawa (2009), Tamai (1992, 1997, 2005), and Yanagihara (1995) instead of the silent-reading activity applied in the studies by Iwashita (2008) and Oyama (2009). According to Kadota (2007), reading aloud is defined as a vocalized version of phonological coding. Under reading aloud conditions—unlike those of silent reading—all of the words must be vocalized (phonologically coded). In vocalizing each word in the text, learners are provided with opportunities to notice the inadequacy of their phonetic knowledge. Furthermore, new methods of shadowing developed by investigating the relationships between reading aloud and shadowing might also allow for the possibility of improving listening comprehension. Therefore, this book will demonstrate new ways of implementing the shadowing method by investigating the relationship between reading aloud and shadowing.

As described earlier, Baddeley (1986) claims that both visual and auditory input share the same encoding process (called the phonological coding process), which is necessary before any higher cognitive processing for comprehension can occur. Tamai (2005) argues that shadowing corresponds to the phonological coding process of auditory input. On the other hand, Kadota (2007) argues that reading aloud corresponds to the phonological coding process of visual input. In short, shadowing and reading aloud can be safely stated to share the phonological coding process. Past research on the shadowing method has included reading aloud. Since reading aloud and shadowing commonly employ the phonological coding process, reading aloud might influence later shadowing performance. In other words, for learners for whom shadowing does not facilitate the phonological coding process, a combination of shadowing and reading aloud might be more effective.

Therefore, this research develops a new shadowing method that effectively combines shadowing and reading aloud by adopting the theoretical framework on the basis of findings involving priming effects. Reading aloud relates to the process of visual input, and shadowing relates to the process of auditory input. In the field of psychology, research on the relationship and interaction between two different types of processing (i.e., reading aloud and shadowing) has employed the priming method. The following section will discuss three issues: what the priming effect is, how much research on the priming method has been done in the field of L2 studies, and how reading aloud relates to shadowing.

Priming Effect (RQ 2)

The priming method is "…[a] predominant experimental paradigm employed to study the cognitive aspects of language learning and use" (Trofimovich & McDonough, 2011, p. 4). The priming effect refers to "a phenomenon in which prior exposure to specific language forms or meanings either facilitate[s] or interferes with a speaker's subsequent language comprehension or production" (Trofimovich & McDonough, 2011, p. 4). The prior exposure is often called a "prime," and the consequences generated by the prime are often called the "target."

For example, under combinations of prime and target such as

"BREAD-BUTTER" or "NURSE-DOCTOR," in which the prime is semantically related to the target, the time necessary to render a lexical decision becomes shorter than that for combinations such as "BREAD-DOCTOR," in which the prime and target are not related semantically (Meyer, & Schvaneveldt, 1971). In this case, processing of the prime word, "BREAD," facilitated processing of the target word, "BUTTER." In the previous example, if the presentation of semantically or phonetically related words is separated by a short period of time (several hundred ms to several s), the processing of the target becomes shorter than under the no-relation condition. This is called the indirect priming effect (Mori, Inoue, & Matsui, 2009).

Again, the priming effect generated by combining words closely related in meaning is called the semantic priming effect. Beyond semantic priming, combining phonetically related words also yields a priming effect (called the phonological priming effect; Mori, Inoue, & Matsui, 2009). Semantic and phonological priming are both referred to as *indirect priming*, since the presented stimuli are not identical. The priming effect also occurs when an identical stimulus is repeatedly presented; this is called *direct priming*. According to Wilding (1986), the combination of indirect and direct priming strengthens the effects. For example, in one study, after the presentation of "BREAD-BUTTER," the participants are asked to perform lexical decision tasks in which they are asked to judge whether presented words are actual words or nonwords. After the prime presentations and lexical decision tasks, the participants repeat the series of tasks. This results in faster reactions to the target than in the first task (Oka, 2000).

As to this phenomenon's mechanism of occurrence, Posner and Snyder (1975) argue that there are two different types of factors driving the priming effect: the first is automatic spreading activation (Collins & Loftus, 1975) in semantic memory, which is considered to be part of the implicit memory that occurs during prime processing. The second factor is control of processing by the learner's attention or expectations. According to Posner and Snyder (1975), the processing of "BREAD-BUTTER" occurs by automatic activation of semantic memory. However, processing the first prime and target will naturally lead participants to expect the same type of word combination in the following trial. In other words, the presentation of "BREAD-BUTTER" becomes the prime, and the processing of the second word pair becomes the target. Then, if the target matches the learner's expectations (in the case that the words semantically relate to each other), the processing time for the target becomes faster; however, if not, the target processing time will be controlled and slower. In this way, the priming effect consists of two different mechanisms: automatic and controlled processing; furthermore, these mechanisms interact with each other. Therefore, in experimental paradigms in the field of cognitive psychology, researchers often manipulate reaction times or the relatedness of the stimuli (Oka, 2000).

　Priming studies involving L2 acquisition have recently appeared in specialized psychology journals (Trofimovich & McDonough, 2011). However, since most priming research in L2 acquisition studies still focuses on theoretical issues, very little research has investigated the application of the priming method in pedagogical settings (Trofimovich & McDonough, 2011). Furthermore, McDonough and Trofimovich (2009) argue for the existence of the following two issues in L2 priming research. First, the variety of tasks given to participants within each category of priming research is limited. For example, auditory priming research mainly employs repetition tasks, semantic priming research primarily uses lexical decision tasks, and syntactic priming research uses script interaction tasks. McDonough and Trofimovich (2009) argue that research on task validity (i.e., choosing which tasks are relevant in L2 acquisition studies) is necessary for the application of priming methods in L2 studies. For example, lexical decision tasks require judgment of whether the words presented visually or verbally are actual words or nonwords. However, such tasks have rarely been practiced in actual language classrooms. Thus, McDonough and Trofimovich (2009) suggest that priming research in L2 studies should choose such tasks as reading aloud or shadowing, which are more familiar to learners than lexical decision tasks and often practiced in the classroom.

Moreover, McDonough and Trofimovich (2009) argue that the current focus of researchers of priming methods is on between- or cross-language priming, in which participants are asked to process a prime in one language and a target in another language. However, little research has been conducted on within-language priming, in which both the primes and targets are presented in the same language. McDonough and Trofimovich (2009) further argue for the necessity of research examining the relationship between visual and auditory inputs within language priming.

Two issues in L2 priming studies were discussed in this section. Past research suggests the necessity of choosing methods relevant to the pedagogical field and of further research on within-language priming.

As stated above, McDonough and Trofimovich (2009) argue that L2 priming studies should choose tasks relevant to learners, and one of the tasks they suggest is shadowing. This method has captured the attention of researchers in L2 studies, especially in Japan. Empirical research has consequently been conducted on the efficacy of shadowing for listening comprehension skills.

Tamai (2005) and Kadota (2007) insist that the shadowing method leads to improvement in the processing of L2 auditory input in the phonological loop within working memory. On the other hand, Ochi (2005) and Tanaka (2004) call for modification of the current shadowing method, since shadowing is too cognitively demanding for novice or lower intermediate levels of students. It is necessary to modify the current shadowing method to adapt it to learners who have gaps between their levels of visual and auditory linguistic knowledge.

According to the perspective of the priming effect, learners' expectations control their shadowing performance. In other words, learners' shadowing performance will be greatly improved if expected material is given to them as a prime. Past research has found two different prime conditions that might facilitate shadowing performance: one is the facilitation of function word processing through modification of auditory input (Koike, 1993; Sudo, 2010); the other is that of filling in the gaps between visual and auditory linguistic information (Field, 2003; Nakayama & Iwata, 2012). Therefore, this research will compare the following two prime conditions to develop a better shadowing method. In one, learners are asked to shadow modified auditory inputs in which the speed and number of weak forms of function words are manipulated. The other prime condition combines visual and auditory input, and learners are asked to shadow both. By comparing these two prime conditions, this research will develop a new shadowing method that facilitates learners' shadowing performance.

This section has discussed what the priming effect is and how much research on the priming method has been conducted in L2 studies. Past research studies suggest that priming effects can cause prior experiences to either facilitate or interfere with subsequent language comprehension or production. Moreover, several different kinds of priming effects exist, while two different forms of processing (automatic and controlled) interact to determine how priming occurs.

Further, the number of past investigations on the priming method in L2 studies is limited, though the topic has captured the attention of L2 studies' researchers. Nevertheless, the focus of these researchers has been limited to how processing of the L1 affects that of the L2. They have not investigated the relationship between two different types of processing (i.e., reading and speaking) in the L2 alone. Furthermore, some of the tasks assigned in previous studies are not relevant to classroom L2 studies. Tasks considered more relevant to L2 studies, such as shadowing or reading aloud, should therefore be applied in subsequent investigations.

On the basis of the past research described above, this book focuses on the relationship between the processing of auditory and visual input in the L2. The studies in this book will adopt reading aloud and shadowing tasks, as suggested by McDonough and Trofimovich (2009). In this research, under the premise that the modality of the presented text affects the learners' comprehension, a new shadowing method is developed to determine the relationships between the processing of visual and auditory inputs in the priming method.

This research incorporates three studies conducted to investigate whether a combination of reading aloud and shadowing facilitates shadowing performance more effectively than other combinations

(Studies 2–4). Study 5 then investigates whether the best method (as revealed by Studies 2–4) improves listening comprehension skills more effectively than the shadowing method that has been applied in past research.

Purpose of This Research

Previous findings suggest that shadowing improves L2 listening comprehension skills, but two unsolved issues remain. First, few studies have investigated whether the shadowing method causes greater improvement in listening comprehension than the methods broadly practiced in current pedagogical settings, or how the effectiveness of these methods differs (RQ 1). Second, though past research on the shadowing method has adopted a combination of reading aloud and shadowing, little research has been conducted on how reading aloud interacts with or affects shadowing performance (RQ 2).

The purpose of this research is to answer RQ 1 and RQ 2 and develop a new shadowing method under the theoretical frameworks of the situation model (Kintsch et al., 1990), language processing, and the priming effect. In Chapter 5, as a first step, the efficacy of the shadowing method adopted in past research is investigated through Study 1. In Chapter 6, a new shadowing method is developed on the basis of the findings of Study 1. Then, in Chapter 7, the efficacy of the novel shadowing method is investigated under a priming paradigm. Finally, in Chapter 8, I summarize the findings of the studies and discuss the implications of the research.

Chapter 5

A Study on the Efficacy of Shadowing Training (Study 1)

Introduction

Self-monitoring strategy refers to a task in which learners evaluate their own shadowing performance by listening to their shadowed voices as soon as they finish each shadowing trial and marking the words successfully shadowed on the transcript (Nakayama & Suzuki, 2012). In this chapter, the efficacy of shadowing training, which includes this self-monitoring strategy, is investigated.

Objective

This study investigates whether the shadowing training procedures suggested by Nakayama and Suzuki (2012) lead to greater improvements in listening comprehension skills than the training procedures widely used in Japanese L2 listening instruction. To do so, it applies the instruction procedures included in four Japanese high school Oral Communication I textbooks approved by MEXT (the Ministry of Education, Culture, Sports, Science and Technology). Furthermore, to determine deeper improvement of listening comprehension skills, this study adopts a listening test based on the model of text comprehension by Kintsch et al. (1990).

By comparing the shadowing method to the widely used listening instructions, we can differentiate how those two methods contribute to listening comprehension. Furthermore, by adopting the model of Kintsch et al. (1990), we can determine whether the shadowing method adopted in this study improves the level of listening comprehension.

The purpose of this study is to investigate whether the shadowing training procedures suggested by Nakayama and Suzuki (2012) lead to greater improvement in listening comprehension skills than the training procedures predominantly used in Japanese L2 listening instruction.

Method

Participants

The participants in this study were 60 university students (male $n = 35$, female $n = 25$) from two English classes. The results of the TOEIC® (Test of English for International Communication) listening practice test, which was conducted prior to the study, showed no significant differences in listening proficiency between the classes ($p > .05$). All participants were native speakers of Japanese, and none had any experience of living in a country where the first or second language is English. They had been participating in a weekly 90-min English course for about 2 months from April until June of 2011 to improve their TOEIC® test-taking techniques.

The two classes were assigned to either a shadowing group (experimental group) or a group receiving instructions adapted from high school English textbooks approved by Ministry of Education, Culture, Sports, Science and Technology, MEXT (control group).

Materials

TOEIC® Practice Test

The TOEIC® practice test was used in this study to measure proficiency in general listening. This test was taken from *TOEIC® Tesuto koushiki mondaishu Vol. 3* (Educational Testing Service, 2008). There were 100 questions in the listening section, and the testing time was approximately 45 min.

Situation Model Listening Comprehension Test

This study employed the situation model listening comprehension test, which was developed by Nakayama et al. (2015). This is a multiple-choice test in which each question is associated with three choices. There were 25 questions in total, based on six short descriptive passages in English. Each of the passages contained between three and five sentences taken from sources such as news media or radio commercials, which were considered comprehensible for the participants if presented visually. There were several questions related to each passage: one asked the listener to describe the topic of the entire passage in Japanese (situation model), then one or two questions asked the listener to choose a statement that was different in terms of description but the same in terms of content as a sentence in the passage (textbase), and then one or two questions required the participant to select a sentence that was exactly the same as one in the passage (surface structure). The following numbers of questions were asked at each representation level: 6, 7, and 12 questions were related to the situation model, textbase, and surface structure, respectively, for a total of 25 questions. All of the passages were read by one native English-speaking male Canadian who had been teaching English at a university in Japan for 7 years at a speech rate of approximately 140 words/min. The reader's voice was recorded on an IC recorder (Olympus Voice-Trek V-22) and then converted into digital audio files. This test took approximately 25 min to administer. An example of a passage and related questions is given in Table 2.

Table 2

Examples of a Passage and Related Questions

Passage:	You can buy two pens and get a third pen for free. Buy six pens and pay only four dollars. If you buy more than 10 pens, we'll give you a free notebook.
Situation model question	足し算の話 (a talk about addition)
	安売りの話 (a talk about a bargain sale)
	買い物リストの話 (a talk about a shopping list)
Textbase question	Buy four pens and pay only six dollars.
	You can get six pens for only four dollars.
	You can get four pens for only six dollars.
Surface structure question	You can buy two pens and get a third pen free.
	If you buy two pens, you can get a third pen free.
	If you buy three pens, you can get one of them free.

Chapter 5   A Study on the Efficacy of Shadowing Training (Study 1)   49

Shadowing Scripts and Audio Materials

The shadowing scripts and audio materials were selected from VOA (Voice of America) Special English and subsequently divided into five lessons. The reason for selecting these materials is that they consisted of 1,500 basic words and were considered comprehensible if presented visually. Each script consisted of 186–211 words. The average presentation speed of all audio materials was 116 words/min. The scripts for each lesson were given as A4-size paper handouts to both groups, and the audio materials were presented using a computer connected to the classroom's PA system.

Teaching Materials for the Control Group

The teaching materials for the control group were based on the same scripts and audio materials as those for the shadowing group, following four high school Oral Communication I English textbooks (Kawabe & Kobashi, 2010; Negishi, Yoshitomi, Kano, Shizuka, & Takayama, 2007; Nomura et al., 2005; Yata, Kohashi, Tamura, & Nishimiya, 2010). Each of the textbooks was approved by MEXT. The teaching materials consisted of four types of questions based on the scripts as follows: Activity 1—a warm-up activity, in which students were asked to write down as many English words relating to a key word given by the instructor as possible; Activity 2—a listening activity in which students were asked to understand the gist of the content; Activity 3—a listening activity in which students were asked to answer three questions about the details of the content; Activity 4—a dictation exercise that asks students to write down the missing words in the script. Activities 3 and 4 consisted of multiple-choice questions in which students were asked to choose the answer from

Activity 1
日本にはどのような祝日がありますか？下の余白に書いてみてください。 (What kinds of holidays exist in Japan? Please write them down in the space below.)

Activity 2	Activity 3
What will people do next week? A) Express their thanks to teachers B) Go to school to see a contest C) Visit the union's web site	How do people express their thanks to teachers? A) Through exchanging gifts B) Through simply saying thank you. C) In many ways

Activity 4
Next week many parents, students, and administrators will (　) their appreciation (　) gifts, cards, flowers, or other special treats. Some schools hold contests in which students (　) about their favorite teachers. The (　) are read at special ceremonies. 　A few years ago, the National Education Association asked (　) what they would most like to (　) in appreciation of their (　). Most said that all they wanted was a simple "(　) (　)."

Figure 1. Example questions assigned to control group.

three choices. Examples of the four activities are shown in Figure 1.

Procedure

The participants took the situation model listening comprehension test and TOEIC® practice test before (pretest) and after (posttest) the training. However, the order of the questions was manipulated for the posttest to exclude learning effects as much as possible. The training sessions were conducted on 5 consecutive weeks, once per week, with each session lasting 60 min. Each training session followed the procedure described in Table 3.

Table 3

Lesson Procedures

Task	Shadowing group		Task	Control group	
1.	Listen to the audio silently	5 min	1.	Activity 1	5 min
2.	Shadowing (3 times)	20 min	2.	Listen to the audio silently	5 min
3.	Reading aloud	5 min	3.	Activity 2 (2 times)	10 min
4.	Reading the script for comprehension	10 min	4.	Activity 3 (2 times)	15 min
5.	Shadowing (3 times)	20 min	5.	Activity 4 (2 times)	15 min
			6.	Checking answers on Activity 4	10 min

Note. *The number in parentheses shows the frequency with which the audio was played.

Training Session in the Shadowing Group

The shadowing group first listened to the auditory text silently for 5 min (Task 1). Afterwards, they engaged in a shadowing task in which the participants were asked to shadow the auditory text to the provided IC recorders. After each trial of shadowing, they were asked to look at the script and underline the words they had successfully shadowed, listening to their shadowed voices on the IC recorders. The participants in the shadowing group repeated these processes three times (Task 2). A period of 20 min was allotted for this activity. After three shadowing trials, the participants were asked to read the script aloud for 5 min (Task 3) and then reread the script for comprehension for 10 min (Task 4). After these two activities, the participants were asked to engage in shadowing following the same process they had used in Task 2 (Task 5).

Training Session in Control Group

The participants were asked to engage in Activity 1 with the intention of this activating their schemata to facilitate their understanding of the audio text (Task 1), with 5 min allotted to this activity. Then, the participants were asked to listen to the audio text silently for 5 min. Next, the participants were asked to engage in Activity 2, which required them to answer multiple-choice questions relating to the main points of the auditory text, having listened to it twice (Task 2), with 10 min allotted to this activity. After Task 2, the participants were required to answer questions asking for more details of the auditory text after listening to it twice (Task 3), with 15 min allotted to this activity. Then, the participants were asked to engage in dictation, which required them to fill in the blanks by writing down the missing words while listening to the auditory text twice (Task 4), with 15 min allotted to this activity. Finally, the participants were asked to check their answers on Task 4, with 10 min allotted for this activity.

Frequency of Listening to Auditory Text between Groups

Both the shadowing and control groups listened to the auditory text six times. The frequency did not differ between the groups.

Scoring

TOEIC® Practice Test

One point was given for each correct answer, with a total of 100 possible points on both the pretest and posttest. The gain score was calculated by subtracting each participant's score on the posttest from that of the pretest in order to ascertain improvement in listening comprehension skills as a result of the experiment.

Situation Model Listening Comprehension Test

One point was given for each correct answer, and the score was calculated as the proportion of correct answers out of the total number of questions on each level. For example, if a participant answered three questions correctly on the surface structure, three was divided by seven (the total number of questions on that level), resulting in a score of 0.43 for the surface structure. This process was conducted for both the pretest and posttest. The scores were grouped according to each representation level for further analysis. Then, the gain score was calculated by subtracting each participant's score on the posttest from that of the pretest in order to ascertain improvement in listening comprehension skills as a result of the experiment.

Analysis

Separate analyses were conducted on the four dependent measures (scores on the TOEIC® practice test, surface structure, textbase, and situation model) in order to examine whether these were differently affected by the two types of listening instructions (for the shadowing vs. control groups). To determine whether there were differences in improvement between the two groups in terms of TOEIC® practice test performance, a Student's t test was performed on the gain scores between groups (i.e., shadowing group vs. control group). To determine if the differences in improvement between the two groups varied across the three representation levels, three sets of Student's t tests were conducted on the gain scores between groups (i.e., shadowing group vs. control group) for each representation level (situation model, textbase, and surface level). All statistical tests were conducted with an α of .05.

Results and Discussion

TOEIC Practice Test

The differences in gain scores between groups were significant ($t(54) = 4.40$, $p < .01$). The average gain score of the shadowing group ($M = 7.68$; $SD = 5.15$) was significantly higher than that of the control group ($M = 0.57$; $SD = 6.81$). The mean scores and standard deviations of both groups and the results of the Student's t test are shown in Table 4.

Table 4

TOEIC Practice Test Scores and the Results of t Tests

	Shadowing group ($n = 28$)			Control group ($n = 28$)			t test result
	Pre	Post	Gain	Pre	Post	Gain	
M	43.39	51.07	7.68	43.00	43.57	0.57	4.40**
SD	7.04	9.28	5.15	9.39	13.15	6.81	

Note. **$p < .01$

Situation Model Listening Comprehension Test

The gain scores of neither situation model nor surface structure were significant between groups, ($t(54) = 0.53$, $p > .05$) and ($t(54) = 0.91$, $p > .05$), respectively. However, according to the Student's t test conducted on the gain scores on the textbase representation level, the average gain score of the shadowing group ($M = 0.48$; $SD = 0.18$) was significantly higher than that of the control group ($M = 0.32$; $SD =$

Table 5

Scores of Situation Model Listening Comprehension Test and the Results of t Tests

		Shadowing group (n = 28)			Control group (n = 28)			
		Pre	Post	Gain	Pre	Post	Gain	
Surface	M	0.53	0.72	0.19	0.47	0.60	0.13	n.s.
	SD	0.16	0.14	0.23	0.18	0.16	0.21	
Textbase	M	0.32	0.48	0.16	0.37	0.32	−0.05	**2.90****
	SD	0.16	0.18	0.24	0.21	0.18	0.30	
Situation	M	0.38	0.44	0.06	0.30	0.39	0.09	n.s.
	SD	0.19	0.17	0.25	0.19	0.19	0.25	

Note. **p < .01

0.18). The mean scores and standard deviations of both groups and the results of the Student's *t* test are shown in Table 5.

The method of shadowing including an activity to supplement self-monitoring can thus improve listening comprehension more than the listening instructions commonly used in Japanese L2 listening pedagogy. However, the results of the situation model listening comprehension tests suggest that the improvement brought about by the method of shadowing adopted in this study might be limited, since significant improvement was identified only at the textbase level. Since the improvement in terms of the situation model, which represents the overall comprehension of a text, did not differ between groups, the shadowing method to supplement self-monitoring does not seem to have been sufficient to improve listening comprehension skills. In other words, the findings of this study suggest that facilitation of the phonological coding process by shadowing alone has limitations with respect to improvement in listening comprehension. Therefore, a better method should be determined to improve listening comprehension at the level of the situation model. The next chapter examines how reading aloud relates to or influences shadowing performance and then establishes a new method including a reading aloud activity to improve listening comprehension in terms of the situation model.

Chapter 6

New Shadowing Training Procedures to Facilitate Overall Understanding of Spoken Texts Based on the Findings of Priming Methods

Introduction

Chapter 5 investigated the efficacy of shadowing training including an activity to supplement self-monitoring while shadowing (cf. Nakayama & Suzuki, 2012). The research findings suggest that shadowing training involving an activity for the supplementation of self-monitoring improved learners' listening comprehension only on the textbase level; it did not improve learners' understanding of the overall meanings of the texts. These findings indicate the necessity of developing a new shadowing method to address this discrepancy. Therefore, in Chapter 6, the relationship between reading aloud and shadowing is investigated from the perspective of priming methods. A better shadowing method intended to improve listening comprehension of the overall meaning of text will be proposed. To accomplish this, first, a method of shadowing with modified auditory input will be compared with the one using regular-speed shadowing material in Section 1 (Study 2).

Second, a combination of reading aloud and shadowing will be compared with the regular shadowing training procedure in Section 2 (Study 3). Then, the research findings of Studies 2 and 3 will be compared in Section 3 (Study 4).

Effectiveness of Modified Auditory Input for Shadowing (Study 2)

Objective

This study investigates whether auditory input considered to conform to learners' prior auditory knowledge might improve their shadowing performance more than auditory input that is more native-like in speed and pronunciation. Pre- and post-training shadowing performance is compared between two groups: the prime group shadowing three auditory input streams with different speeds and numbers of weak forms (Level 1: very slow with no weak forms; Level 2: slow with some weak forms; and Level 3: natural speed with the most weak forms); and the control group repeating shadowing on the Level 3 material.

Method

Participants
The participants in this study were 26 first-year university students who were enrolled in the author's English language course. All the participants were native speakers of Japanese. None had any experience of living in a country in which English is the first or second

language. They had been participating in the English course for 90 minutes once a week for about 2 months with the purpose of improving their TOEIC test-taking techniques. The students were assigned to one of two groups. The prime group and the control group each comprised 13 participants.

Materials

Shadowing script and audio materials. For the shadowing script, "Job Market: An Extra Hard Test for New College Graduates" was selected from VOA Special English (VOA), from which 274 words were excerpted (out of a total of 508 words in the original version), consisting of 80 function words and 194 content words. The passage was recorded by a Canadian L2 instructor who had lived in Japan for 8 years. The recordings were made with an IC recorder (Sony ICX-UX71) and converted into MP3 files in order to present them via a computer connected to a PA system in the classroom. After 11 recording trials, 3 recordings that varied in speed and number of the weak forms of function words were chosen by the instructor and the author. The speed and number of the weak forms of function words in the selected recordings are shown in Table 6. The transcript of each presented recording was given to both groups as A4-size paper handouts.

Table 6

The Proportions of the Numbers of Weak Forms and Speech Speeds of the Three Recordings

		Level 1	Level 2	Level 3
Proportion of weak forms		0.00	0.38	0.96
Speech speed (words/s)	*M*	0.61	1.04	1.96
	SD	0.11	0.16	0.54

Procedure

Pretest

After the author explained the objective and outline of the study, an IC recorder was provided for each participant. Following a demonstration of shadowing by the author (cf. Nakayama & Suzuki, 2012), the participants were asked to shadow the audio of Level 3 and record their shadowed voices on the IC recorders prior to the training session.

Training Session

Experimental group (prime group). Participants in the prime group were asked to shadow three different audio samples, from Level 1 to 3. In each trial, participants were asked to record their shadowed voices on the IC recorders. After each trial, they were asked to underline the shadowed words by pencil on the transcript sheets while listening to their own recorded shadowed voices. Participants in the prime group engaged in three shadowing trials.

Control group. Participants in the control group were asked to shadow the Level 3 audio three times. The procedure was identical between groups apart from the different patterns of audio sample presentation.

Posttest

After the training session, all participants were asked to shadow the Level 3 audio and record their shadowed voices on IC recorders, following the same procedure as on the pretest.

Scoring

Various methods of evaluating shadowing performance exist. For example, Tamai (2005) suggests so-called "syllable evaluation" and "check point evaluation." In syllable evaluation, a marker listens to the shadowed voice to check whether each syllable has been pronounced correctly. Since the syllable is the basic unit of written and spoken language, this can be precisely evaluated. However, syllable evaluation requires intensive concentration to evaluate the speech. This type of evaluation can become unstable according to the evaluator's level of fatigue (Shimomura, Minematsu, Yamauchi, & Hirose, 2008). On the other hand, check point evaluation poses a lighter burden on the marker. In the check point method, words set according to a certain pattern prior to the experiment are marked by markers. A high correlation between check point evaluation and syllable evaluation was demonstrated by Tamai (2005); however, some issues are inherent in these two evaluation methods. For example, in syllable evaluation, even if the word "be·cause" is mistaken as "be·come," the participant will receive 1 point out of 2, though these two words are completely different in meaning. In check point evaluation, no clear guidelines have been set on which words should be included in the evaluation (Shimomura et al., 2008).

An alternative method to evaluate shadowing performance is called the "all words evaluation method." In this method, every word in the script is evaluated (Shimomura et al., 2008). The all-words evaluation method can address the two issues mentioned above. First, the all words evaluation method poses less burden on the marker than syllable evaluation, so it may be more stable than the latter. Furthermore, since it is not syllables but words that are the targets in the all words evaluation method, the issue elucidated by Shimomura et al. (2008) can be avoided. Moreover, in the all words evaluation method, guidelines on evaluation procedures are much clearer than those for check point evaluation. Therefore, this study adopted all words evaluation, as in Nakayama and Suzuki (2012).

Results and Discussion

The author listened to the recordings of each participant's pretest and posttest shadowing and checked them against a transcript of the actual passage. Although any words that were incorrect, omitted, or inserted are normally counted as errors, insertion was ignored in this study. Across the experiments reported here, data from 6 participants (10%) were re-coded by a second rater. The correlation between the total number of errors detected by the coders was 0.94. One point was given for each correctly shadowed word, with a total possible score of 274 points (in the case of all words being shadowed correctly). After both the pretest and posttest were scored, the scores were sorted into the two word groups: function words (80 words) and content words

(194 words).

Gain Scores within Word Groups between Pretest and Posttest

Following Kikuchi and Nakayama (2006), the gain scores between pretest and posttest were calculated by the following procedures. First, the number of successfully shadowed words was calculated for each participant at both pretest and posttest, subdivided by word groups. Then, the scores were converted into proportions according to Formulae 1 and 2.

Formula 1: number of successfully shadowed function words / total number of function words (80 words in total)

Formula 2: number of the successfully shadowed content words / total number of content words (194 words in total)

Homogeneity between groups at pretest

To confirm homogeneity between groups at pretest, a two-way ANOVA was conducted, with group (the prime group vs. the control group) as a between-subject variable and the two word groups (function words and content words) as within-subject variables. The analysis revealed no significant differences between groups ($F(1, 24) = 1.07$, $p > .05$), thereby confirming that there was no difference in shadowing performance between groups at the pretest stage. Then, the gain score was calculated according to Formulae 3 and 4.

Formula 3: proportion of successfully shadowed function words at posttest − proportion of successfully shadowed function words at pretest = gain score of function words

Formula 4: proportion of successfully shadowed content words at posttest − proportion of successfully shadowed content words at pretest = gain score of content words

Then, to determine the improvement between groups, a two-way ANOVA was conducted, with group (the prime group vs. the control group) as a between-subject variable and the two word groups (function words and content words) as within-subjects variables. Table 7 presents the mean scores of the pretest, posttest, and gain scores. There were no significant differences either between groups or word groups, ($F(1, 24) = 0.05$, $p > .05$) and ($F(1, 24) = 3.42$, $p > .05$), respectively. However, the interaction between group and word group was significant ($F(1, 24) = 4.32$, $p < .05$). The simple main effect of group was significant when the data were restricted to function words only ($F(1, 47) = 7.60$, $p < .01$). According to Tukey's Honestly Significant Difference (HSD) test, the gain scores of function words in the prime group ($M = 0.17$, $SD = 0.09$) were significantly higher than those in the control group ($M = 0.08$, $SD = 0.07$) ($t(25) = 3.90$, $p < .01$). The simple main effect of word group was significant for neither the prime group ($F(1, 24) = 2.66$, $p > .10$) nor the control group ($F(1, 24) = 0.20$, $p > .10$).

The findings of this study suggest that shadowing training with the modified audio method applied in this study might better facilitate shadowing performance on function words than the regular shadowing method. However, since there was no difference between the gain scores on function words and content words in the prime group, further research needs to be done to investigate the reliability of this method.

Table 7

Pretest, Posttest, and Gain Scores in Word Groups Between Groups

Word groups/methods		The prime group (N=48)			The control group (N=47)		
		Pre	Post	Gain	Pre	Post	Gain
Function words	(*M*)	0.23	0.40	0.17	0.19	0.27	0.08
	(*SD*)	0.13	0.13	0.09	0.15	0.14	0.07
Content words	(*M*)	0.46	0.58	0.12	0.46	0.59	0.12
	(*SD*)	0.15	0.13	0.09	0.11	0.08	0.10

Note. The numbers indicate proportions.

Previous findings (Field, 2003; Koike, 1993; Nakayama & Iwata, 2012; Sudo, 2010) suggest that Japanese EFL learners tend to have difficulty in decoding weak forms of function words in listening conditions. This study confirmed that the adopted modified audio shadowing method might facilitate shadowing performance better than the shadowing method applied in past research.

Effectiveness of Combination of Reading Aloud and Shadowing (Study 3)

Objective

This study investigates whether a shadowing training procedure that combines reading aloud and shadowing yields better shadowing performance than the regular shadowing training procedure, which repeats shadowing only. Shadowing requires so-called on-line processing of auditory input, which requires listening and repetition at the same time. On the other hand, reading aloud requires so-called off-line processing of visual input, which requires learners to read text aloud at their own pace. To create a similar condition to shadowing, this study adopts a new reading aloud procedure called the visual shadowing procedure, which requires learners to read text aloud employing on-line processing. Pre- and post-training shadowing performance is compared among the three groups: a group engaging in both visual and auditory shadowing, a group engaging in only visual shadowing, and a control group, in which learners are asked to repeat auditory shadowing.

The visual shadowing procedure asks learners to repeat sentences that successively appear and then disappear on the screen according to their actual utterance times. It does not allow learners to reprocess the text, similar to the shadowing condition. Then, the prime condition (in which visual and auditory shadowing are repeated) and the control conditions (in which only visual shadowing is repeated or, only auditory shadowing is repeated) are compared in terms of shadowing performance. The purpose of this study is to investigate which of the shadowing training procedures—visual-auditory shadowing, visual shadowing or auditory shadowing—best improves shadowing performance.

Method

Participants

The participants were 65 university students (males $n = 43$, females $n = 22$), all of whom were native speakers of Japanese. None had any experience of living in a country whose first or second language is

English. They had been participating in a weekly 90-min English course for about 2 months from April until June of 2010 to improve their TOEIC® test-taking techniques.

The students were placed into groups of equal listening proficiency according to the results of the TOEIC® practice test conducted prior to this study; 22 students were selected for the visual-auditory shadowing group (VAS group; $M = 40.4$; $SD = 4.47$), another 21 students were placed in the visual shadowing group (VS group; $M = 39.57$; $SD = 5.26$), and the other 22 students were placed in the auditory shadowing group (AS group; $M = 39.00$; $SD = 4.29$). A one-way ANOVA confirmed that there were no significant differences in listening proficiency among the groups ($F(2, 64) = 0.53$, $p > .05$).

Materials

TOEIC® Practice Test

The same TOEIC® practice test given in Study 1 was also employed in this study to measure the participants' general listening proficiency.

Shadowing Scripts and Audio Materials

A speech about 3D printers was chosen as the shadowing script and audio material for this study. This speech was recorded by an American man at a speech rate of 114.6 words/min (219 total words). The transcript was given as A4-size paper handouts to both groups.

PowerPoint Slides for Visual Shadowing

PowerPoint slides were created from the shadowing script for visual shadowing by the VAS and VS groups. Initially, the speed of each sentence in the script was calculated by dividing the total number of words by the total time taken for the sentence to be spoken, in accordance with Takefuta (1984). The author then created one slide for each sentence, and the presentation duration of the slide was adjusted according to the sentence speed. Since the script comprised 21 sentences, 21 slides were developed containing a single sentence per slide as well as a title page, yielding 22 slides in total. The first sentence of the script was spoken in 5 s; thus, the slide for the sentence was

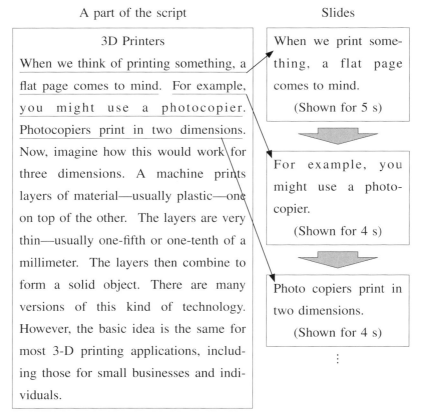

Figure 2. Examples of PowerPoint slides for visual shadowing.

shown for 5 s. Examples of slides and the presentation procedure are shown in Figure 2.

Pretest

After the author outlined the study and explained its objectives, an IC recorder was provided for each participant. After a demonstration of shadowing by the author (cf. Nakayama & Suzuki, 2012), the participants were asked to shadow the audio material and record their shadowed voices on the IC recorders prior to the training session.

Training session
VAS group. Following the demonstration of voice shadowing, the participants were shown the PowerPoint slides and given an explanation and demonstration of visual shadowing; then, they were asked to undertake voice shadowing and visual shadowing on an alternating basis. The author also asked the students to record their voices on the IC recorders and then listen to the recordings immediately after each trial, underlining the shadowed words directly on the transcripts. The participants were asked to follow this procedure in each trial. The experiment consisted of three voice shadowing and three visual shadowing trials, yielding a total of six shadowing assignments.

VS group. Following the demonstration of voice shadowing, the participants were shown the PowerPoint slides and given an explanation and demonstration of visual shadowing before they were asked to undertake voice and visual shadowing. The author then asked the participants to perform voice shadowing while recording their own voices on the IC recorder, listen to the recordings immediately after each trial, and underline the shadowed words on the transcripts. As

Table 8

Lesson Procedures

VAS group	VS group	AS group
Listening	Listening	Listening
Auditory	Visual	Auditory
Visual	Visual	Auditory
Auditory	Visual	Auditory
Visual	Visual	Auditory
Auditory	Visual	Auditory
Visual	Visual	Auditory

with the VAS group, the VS group was instructed to follow the described procedure in each subsequent trial. The participants in the VS group conducted visual shadowing six times in total.

AS group. Following the demonstration of voice shadowing, a second demonstration was given in order to counterbalance that given under the VAS group procedure. The participants were then asked to undertake voice shadowing while recording their own voices on the IC recorders, listen to the recordings immediately after each trial, and underline the shadowed words on the transcripts. Like the VAS group, the AS group was instructed to follow the described procedure in each subsequent trial. The participants in the AS group conducted voice shadowing six times in total. The lesson procedure for each group is described in Table 8.

Posttest

After the training session and pretest procedure, all participants were asked to shadow the audio and record their shadowed voices on the IC recorders.

Table 9

Pretest, Posttest, and Gain Scores in Word Groups

Word groups / Method		VAS			VS			AS		
		Pre	Post	Gain	Pre	Post	Gain	Pre	Post	Gain
Function words	(M)	0.32	0.57	0.25	0.27	0.46	0.19	0.22	0.37	0.15
	(SD)	0.18	0.2	0.12	0.16	0.20	0.11	0.14	0.18	0.09
Content words	(M)	0.57	0.77	0.20	0.5	0.69	0.19	0.48	0.67	0.19
	(SD)	0.16	0.14	0.10	0.14	0.16	0.08	0.11	0.09	0.09

Scoring

Scoring was conducted according to the procedure described in Study 2. The mean scores and standard deviations of the three groups and the gain scores are shown in Table 9.

Results and Discussion

A two-way ANOVA was conducted on the pretest TOEIC® scores to confirm the homogeneity between groups at pretest, with group (VAS, VS, and AS) as a between-subjects variable and the two word groups (function words and content words) as within-subjects variables. The analysis revealed no significant differences between the groups ($F(2, 62) = 2.75$, $p > .05$). Thus, the analysis failed to confirm any differences in shadowing performance between the groups at the pretest stage. Then, the gain scores were calculated according to the same procedure described in Study 2.

Next, a two-way ANOVA was conducted to determine the improvement between the groups, with group (VAS, VS, and AS) as the between-subjects variable and the two word groups (function words and content words) as within-subjects variables. Table 9 presents the mean pretest, posttest, and gain scores. There were no significant differences either between the groups or the word groups ($F(2, 62) = 2.41$, $p > .05$) and ($F(1, 62) = 0.06$, $p > .05$), respectively. However, the interaction between group and word group was significant ($F(2, 62) = 3.88$, $p < .05$). The simple main effect of group was significant when the analysis was restricted to function words only ($F(2, 110) = 5.72$, $p < .05$). According to Tukey's HSD test, the gain scores for function words in the VAS group ($M = 0.25$, $SD = 0.12$) were significantly higher than those of the VS group ($M = 0.19$, $SD = 0.11$) ($t(64) = 2.61$, $p < .05$) and the AS group ($M = 0.15$, $SD = 0.09$) ($t(64) = 4.77$, $p < .01$). The simple main effect of word group was significant for the VAS group only ($F(1, 62) = 4.73$, $p < .05$). According to Tukey's HSD test, the VAS group's gain score for function words ($M = 0.25$, $SD = 0.12$) was significantly larger than for content words ($M = 0.20$, $SD = 0.10$) ($t(64) = 3.74$, $p < .01$). This study's findings suggest that the applied visual-auditory shadowing method facilitates shadowing performance on function words compared with the other two investigated methods.

This study has investigated which of the three prime conditions—reading aloud and shadowing (visual and auditory shadowing), reading aloud (visual shadowing) only, and shadowing only—best facilitates shadowing performance. The results suggest that the visual-auditory shadowing condition facilitates the best shadowing performance for function words. This indicates that the facilitation of processing of visual input by reading aloud might become a prime for the processing of auditory input.

Comparison of Shadowing Performance with Different Primes (Study 4)

Objective

In Studies 2 and 3, two different primes were compared to the shadowing procedure adopted in past research. In Study 2, the prime group that shadowed three auditory passages differing in speed and number of weak forms showed better shadowing performance than the control group. In Study 3, the prime group that repeated both visual and auditory shadowing showed better shadowing performance than the other groups. This study will compare those two primes to investigate which leads to better shadowing performance after training.

Method

Participants
The participants in this study were 95 first-year university students who were enrolled in the author's English language courses. All participants were native speakers of Japanese. None had any experience of living in a country whose first or second language is English. They had been participating in a weekly 90-min English course for about 2 months from April until June of 2010 to improve their TOEIC® test-taking techniques.

The students were assigned to one of the following two groups: a visual-auditory shadowing group (VAS group) comprising 48 participants, and a scaffolded auditory shadowing group (SA group) composed of 47 students. The results of the listening comprehension test administered prior to this experiment revealed no significant differences in listening comprehension between the two groups ($t(93) = 0.03$, $p > .05$).

Materials

The same materials used in Study 2 were also employed in this study. The materials for visual shadowing were created following the same procedure described in Study 3.

Procedure

Pretest and posttest. For pretest and posttest, all the participants were asked to shadow the Level 3 audio and to record their shadowed voices on IC recorders.

Training session. Training was conducted in the same classroom used in the other studies, which was capable of holding 156 students and was outfitted with a PA system. Each lesson took 60 min. The author conducted all lessons for both groups, and the following procedures were undertaken for each of the two groups. Table 10 contains an overview of the procedures.

VAS group. The participants were asked to perform voice shadowing and visual shadowing three times, respectively, thereby yielding a total of six shadowing assignments, as in Study 3.

SA group. The participants were asked to shadow each audio passage twice for a total of six shadowing assignments.

Table 10

Lesson Procedures

VAS group	SA group
Listening	Listening
Auditory	Level 1
Visual	Level 1
Auditory	Level 2
Visual	Level 2
Auditory	Level 3
Visual	Level 3

Table 11

Pretest, Posttest, and Gain Scores in Word Groups Between Groups

Word group/Method		VAS group			SA group		
		Pre	Post	Gain	Pre	Post	Gain
Function words	(M)	0.25	0.49	0.24	0.25	0.44	0.19
	(SD)	0.17	0.19	0.09	0.22	0.22	0.12
Content words	(M)	0.39	0.60	0.21	0.40	0.60	0.20
	(SD)	0.13	0.15	0.09	0.17	0.14	0.10

Note. *The numbers indicate proportions.

Scoring

The scoring was conducted according to the same procedure applied in Study 2. The mean scores and standard deviations of both groups as well as the gain scores are shown in Table 11.

Results and Discussion

A two-way ANOVA was conducted to confirm the homogeneity between the groups at pretest, with group (VAS and SA) as a between-subjects variable and the two word groups (function words and content words) as within-subjects variables. The analysis revealed no significant differences between groups ($F(1, 93) = 0.17$, $p > .05$). The analysis confirmed that there were no differences in shadowing performance between groups at the pretest stage. Then, the gain scores were calculated according to the same procedure described in Study 2.

A two-way ANOVA was conducted to determine the improvement between groups, with group (VAS and SA) as a between-subjects variable and the gain scores for the two word groups (function words and content words) as within-subject variables. There was no significant main effect of group ($F(1, 93) = 2.66$, $p > .05$) or word group ($F(1, 93) = 0.69$, $p > .05$). However, the interaction between group and word group was significant ($F(1, 93) = 4.35$, $p < .05$). The simple main effect of group was significant when the analysis was restricted to function words only ($F(1, 186) = 6.49$, $p < .05$). According to Tukey's HSD test, the VAS group ($M = 0.24$, $SD = 0.09$) outperformed the SA group ($M = 0.19$, $SD = 0.12$) ($t(94) = 3.60$, $p < .01$). The simple main effect of word group was significant for the VAS group only ($F(1, 93) = 4.30$, $p < .05$). According to Tukey's HSD test, the gain score for function words ($M = 0.24$, $SD = 0.09$) was significantly larger than for content words ($M = 0.21$, $SD = 0.09$) in the VAS group ($t(93) = 2.91$, $p < .01$). Table 12 presents the mean pretest, posttest, and gain scores. The findings suggest that the visual-auditory shadowing method applied in this study facilitates better shadowing performance on function words than the scaffolded audio shadowing method.

This study investigated which of two conditions better facilitates shadowing performance—that of the modified speeded audio method or of the visual auditory shadowing method. The findings suggest that the visual-auditory shadowing method better facilitates shadowing performance than the modified speeded audio method. This result confirms that facilitating the processing of visual input prior to the processing of auditory input can facilitate the later processing of auditory input, especially for learners who are better at processing visual than auditory input.

Summary

In this chapter, two prime conditions were compared to develop a new shadowing method. One prime condition employed scaffolded auditory input, and the other was a visual-auditory shadowing condition, which combined reading aloud and shadowing. Those two prime conditions yielded better shadowing performance than the controlled conditions (Studies 2 and 3). However, the visual-auditory shadowing condition yielded better shadowing performance than in the condition in which learners shadowed modified auditory input (Study 4). The efficacy of visual-auditory shadowing procedures is compared with that of the shadowing procedure applied in past research in the next chapter.

Chapter 7

Efficacy of Visual-auditory Shadowing for Listening Comprehension (Study 5)

Introduction

The findings of Study 4 suggest that the prime of visual-auditory shadowing procedures can improve shadowing performance more than that of the scaffolded auditory procedure. However, whether the visual-auditory shadowing training method actually leads to better performance in listening comprehension is still unknown. Therefore, this study investigates whether the visual-auditory shadowing training method better improves L2 listening comprehension than the shadowing method adopted in past research.

Method

Participants

The participants in this study were 67 university students (male $n = 57$, female $n = 10$) who were enrolled in the author's English language courses. All participants were native speakers of Japanese. None had any experience of living in a country in which English is the first or second language. They had been participating in a weekly 90-min English course for about 2 months from April until June of 2011 to improve their TOEIC® test-taking techniques.

The students were assigned to one of two groups: a visual-auditory shadowing group (VAS group), in which participants (male $n = 25$, female $n = 8$) repeated visual and auditory shadowing, or an auditory shadowing group (AS group), in which participants repeated auditory shadowing only (male $n = 32$, female $n = 2$). All participants in each group were asked to record their shadowed voices on IC recorders and to listen to the recordings while reading the transcript. This followed the method used by Nakayama and Suzuki (2012), who indicated that the opportunity to study a transcript and one's own shadowed voice between shadowing tasks (voice feedback) facilitates auditory shadowing.

Materials

TOEIC® practice test
The same TOEIC® practice test used in Study 1 was employed in this

study to measure the participants' proficiency in general L2 listening comprehension.

Shadowing scripts and audio materials

The shadowing scripts and audio materials used for both the VAS and AS groups were created on the basis of those used in Study 1, in which three scripts and audio materials were selected from VOA Special English (VOA) and subsequently divided into five lessons. The reason for selecting these materials is that they each consisted of 1,500 basic words and were considered comprehensible if presented visually. Each script consisted of 186–211 words. The average presentation speed of all the audio materials was 116 words/min. The scripts for each lesson were given as A4-size paper handouts to both groups. The audio materials were presented using a computer connected to the PA system in the classroom.

PowerPoint slides for visual shadowing

For the VAS group's visual shadowing, PowerPoint slides were created from the five shadowing scripts following the method employed in Study 3.

Situation model listening comprehension test

The situation model listening comprehension test developed and used in Study 1 was undertaken in this study.

Procedure

Training of each group took place from the beginning of June to the middle of July 2011. The lessons were given on different days but in the same classroom. Each lesson took 60 min. The author conducted all lessons for both groups, and the following procedures were undertaken for each of the two groups.

Common procedures for both groups

Both groups received the same instructions and demonstrations for the first lesson. First, the participants were asked to sit with sufficient space between them so that each student could concentrate fully on the task without any distraction or disruption from the voices of others. Each participant was given an IC recorder and the script for the lesson. None of the students had prior experience in auditory shadowing, so the technique was explained and demonstrated to them. They were then asked to carry out these instructions when completing the remaining lessons. From that point onward, the VAS and AS groups received different instructions and followed different procedures. The lesson procedures for each group is described in Table 12.

Table 12

Lesson Procedures

Visual-auditory shadowing group (VAS group)	Auditory shadowing group (AS group)
Auditory shadowing	Auditory shadowing
Visual shadowing	Auditory shadowing
Auditory shadowing	Auditory shadowing
Visual shadowing	Auditory shadowing
Auditory shadowing	Auditory shadowing
Visual shadowing	Auditory shadowing

VAS group

Following the demonstration of voice shadowing, the participants were shown the PowerPoint slides and given an explanation and demonstration of visual shadowing; then, they were asked to undertake voice and visual shadowing on an alternating basis. The author also asked the students to record their voices using the IC recorders, listen to the recordings immediately after each trial, and underline the shadowed words on the script sheets. The participants were asked to follow this procedure in three voice shadowing and three visual shadowing trials for a total of six shadowing assignments per lesson.

AS group

Following the demonstration of voice shadowing, a second demonstration was given to the AS group in order to counterbalance the VAS group process. The participants were then asked to undertake voice shadowing and record their voices on the IC recorders, listen to the recordings immediately after each trial, and underline the shadowed words on the script sheets. As in the case of the VAS group, the AS group was instructed to follow the described procedure in each subsequent trial. The participants in the AS group conducted voice shadowing six times per lesson.

Pretest and posttest

Following Study 1, two types of listening tests were administered in this experiment: the TOEIC® practice test and the situation model listening comprehension test. Each test was administered to the participants twice: before the first lesson and after the final lesson. Because the testing sessions were lengthy, a 10-min break was given between the tests.

Scoring

TOEIC® practice test

The scoring procedure in this study was the same as that described in Study 1.

Situation model listening comprehension test

The scoring procedure in this study was also the same as that described in Study 1.

Results and Discussion

Following the procedure in Study 1, separate analyses were conducted on the four dependent measures (the TOEIC practice test, surface structure, textbase, and situation model) in order to examine whether they were differently affected by the two types of listening instructions.

In order to determine whether there were improvements between the two groups in terms of performance on the TOEIC® practice test, a Student's *t* test was performed on the gain scores between groups (VAS group and AS group). In order to determine whether or not there were improvements between the two groups and three representation levels, three sets of Student's *t* tests were conducted on the gain scores between groups for each representation level (the situation model, propositional textbase, and surface level). All statistical tests

Table 13

Scores on TOEIC Practice Tests and the Results of t Tests

	VAS group ($n = 33$)			AS group ($n = 34$)			t test result
	Pre	Post	Gain	Pre	Post	Gain	
M	36.63	41.85	5.21	35.89	37.12	1.24	2.23**
SD	7.31	7.10	6.50	6.49	7.48	8.03	

Note. **$p < .01$.

were conducted with an α of .05.

TOEIC® Practice Test

The differences in gain scores between groups were significant ($t(65) = 2.23$, $p < .05$). The average gain score of the VAS group ($M = 5.21$; $SD = 6.50$) was significantly higher than that of the AS group ($M = 1.24$; $SD = 8.03$). The mean scores and standard deviations of both groups and the results of the Student's t test are shown in Table 13.

Situation Model Listening Comprehension Test

The differences in gain scores between groups were not significant for either the textbase or surface structure, ($t(65) = 1.42$, $p > .05$) and ($t(65) = 0.40$, $p > .05$), respectively. However, according to the Student's t test conducted on the gain scores for the situation model, the average gain score of the VAS group ($M = 0.11$; $SD = 0.17$) was significantly higher than that of the AS group ($M = -0.02$; $SD = 0.18$) ($t(65) = 2.93$, $p < .01$). This suggests that visual-auditory shad-

Table 14

Listening Comprehension Test Scores for the Situation Model and the Results of t Tests

		VAS group ($n = 33$)			AS group ($n = 34$)			t test result
		Pre	Post	Gain	Pre	Post	Gain	
Surface	M	0.44	0.50	0.06	0.47	0.51	0.04	0.40
	SD	0.03	0.17	0.18	0.02	0.13	0.20	
Textbase	M	0.31	0.39	0.09	0.36	0.36	0.00	1.42
	SD	0.03	0.20	0.24	0.02	0.21	0.24	
Situation	M	0.32	0.42	0.11	0.31	0.29	−0.02	2.93**
	SD	0.03	0.18	0.17	0.02	0.15	0.18	

Note. **$p < .01$

owing training improves listening comprehension more than auditory shadowing training alone. The mean scores and standard deviations of both groups and the results of the Student's t test are shown in Table 14.

The present study utilized visually comprehensible materials to investigate whether or not visual-auditory shadowing improves listening comprehension better than auditory shadowing alone. The results revealed the advantages of visual-auditory shadowing training for the improvement of listening comprehension among L2 learners.

The findings of the general listening comprehension tests confirmed that participants' levels of English listening comprehension did not differ between the two groups prior to the experiment and that the English listening comprehension ability of the visual-auditory shadowing group was significantly improved compared with that of the auditory shadowing group after the experiment. The results suggest that visual-auditory shadowing training confers an advantage in listening comprehension compared with auditory shadowing training.

Furthermore, the results of the situation model listening comprehension tests provide some insight into the reason why visual-auditory shadowing training yielded better improvements in listening comprehension than auditory shadowing alone. Analysis of the situation model listening comprehension tests revealed that only the visual-auditory shadowing group showed improvement in comprehension at the situation model level. Kintsch et al. (1990) indicated that the situation model describes the highest level of comprehension, regarding it as the goal of text comprehension. In Study 1, auditory shadowing training did not facilitate cognitive processing sufficiently to reach the situation model level. Our results suggest that visual-auditory shadowing training may generate a deeper understanding of auditory text than the currently practiced shadowing method. Moreover, considering the results of Study 4 and Tamai (2005), the superior performance elicited by visual-auditory shadowing training can likely be explained by the following processes: (1) matching between visual and auditory input by visual-auditory shadowing training facilitates the learning of phonetic variations, (2) learning phonetic variations improves the phonological coding process, and (3) improvement of the phonological coding process frees more attentional resources for higher cognitive processing for enhanced comprehension. These processes show that the facilitation of phonological learning by visual-auditory shadowing is indirectly connected to improvement in listening comprehension. In other words, visual-auditory shadowing does not directly improve listening comprehension, but it facilitates the higher cognitive processing necessary for listening comprehension.

Chapter 8

Conclusion

Summary

This research has verified the effectiveness of shadowing method adopted in past research on L2 learners whose mother tongue phonologically differs from their L2; further, through five studies, it has documented the development of a new shadowing method that is easier for learners to approach and more effective in improving listening comprehension. This book presents methods based on two research frameworks—the text comprehension model developed by Kintsh et al. (1990) and priming methods—to investigate two research questions derived from past findings. First, conclusions will be drawn with respect to the two research questions on the basis of the five studies described herein. Then, the pedagogical implications of the results will be discussed. Finally, directions for future research will be identified.

RQ 1: At which level of understanding is the shadowing method especially effective, and if so how does shadowing differ in effectiveness from the listening instruction mainly practiced in pedagogical settings?

Study 1 investigated at which levels of understanding the shadowing method is especially effective and how shadowing differs in effectiveness from the listening instruction mainly practiced in pedagogical settings. Study 1 adopted the shadowing method broadly accepted in past research and the listening instruction approved by MEXT, which has generally been practiced throughout Japan. It compared participants' listening comprehension performance before and after training. The results suggest that the shadowing method can better improve listening comprehension skills than the widely used method of listening instruction. However, the improvements gained by the shadowing method did not reach the level of overall understanding of the text.

RQ 2: Is a new shadowing method that reinforces the phonological coding process by combining shadowing and reading aloud more effective than the shadowing method currently practiced in pedagogical settings in terms of shadowing performance and comprehension?

Based on the findings of Study 1, a new shadowing method that supports the phonological coding process by combining shadowing and reading aloud was developed in Studies 2–4, and its efficacy was investigated in Study 5. Before studying the combination of shadowing and reading aloud, Study 2 compared shadowing performance using a phased speeded audio method, which scaffolded learners' cognitive load by adjusting reading speed and the number of weak forms of function words, and the shadowing method adopted in past research. The phased speeded audio method adopted in this study yielded better shadowing performance, especially for function words, than the shadowing method that required participants to engage in repeat shadowing of the audio with the fastest speed. Study 3 investigated whether the visual-auditory shadowing method (in which learners alternate between shadowing and reading aloud) better facilitates shadowing performance than the visual shadowing method (in which learners only repeat reading aloud) or the shadowing method (in which learners only repeat shadowing). The results showed that visual-auditory shadowing facilitated shadowing performance the most of all three conditions. Further, the visual-auditory shadowing method facilitated shadowing of function words. Then, Study 4 compared shadowing performance between the phased speeded audio shadowing method and the visual-auditory shadowing method. The findings of Study 4 suggested that the visual-auditory shadowing method better facilitates shadowing performance, especially on weak forms of function words, than the phased speeded audio shadowing method. Finally, Study 5 confirmed that the visual-auditory shadowing method actually yields better improvement in listening comprehension than the shadowing method adopted in past research. The findings suggest that visual-auditory shadowing is not only better at improving listening comprehension but also better at facilitating an overall understanding of the text than the shadowing method adopted in past research.

Implications for Pedagogy

This research has two implications for the field of pedagogy. First, the findings confirmed that the text comprehension model of van Dijk and Kintsch (1983) can be adopted to measure listening comprehension. This is a novel and remarkable finding in L2 listening research. Although standardized instruments to measure L2 listening comprehension, such as the TOEFL® (Test of English as a Foreign Language) and TOEIC® are popular in Japan, these tests provide no deeper analysis. On the other hand, this research proved the possibility of such deeper analysis by using the instrument adopted from van Dijk and Kintsch (1983) to find methods more effective for learners' particular needs, further combining this with other models of language processing such as that of Baddeley (1986).

The second implication of this research is that reading comprehension skills can scaffold (or help to facilitate) listening comprehension skills. The visual-auditory shadowing method, which is a combination of reading aloud and the shadowing method, yielded better improvement in listening comprehension than the shadowing method in which learners only repeat auditory shadowing. The revelation that reading aloud can help to improve listening comprehension could have an impact on L2 reading and listening research, since there has been a long debate on whether or not reading aloud should be encouraged in L2 studies, even including L2 reading classes (Amer, 1997).

Future Research

The efficacy of visual-auditory shadowing training might be limited. The authors chose materials (for shadowing tasks and the situation model listening comprehension test) that the participants could comprehend if presented visually. Whether visual-auditory shadowing training is effective for learning new vocabulary is unknown. It is also unknown whether advanced listeners who have already mastered phonetic variations can replicate these performance improvements, since their phonological coding of auditory input might already have developed enough to allocate attentional resources to listening comprehension.

A further direction for future research is to compare the efficacy of the visual-auditory shadowing method with that of the parallel reading method that was not adopted in this research. Following previous findings, this book developed a visual-auditory shadowing method in which learners alternate between reading aloud and shadowing instead of adopting parallel reading (which was considered too cognitively demanding, as it asks learners to listen to and read the text at the same time). Since the number of available studies on parallel reading is still limited, efficacy comparisons between the visual-auditory shadowing method and the parallel reading method might generate further insights into L2 listening research.

References

Amer, A. (1997). The effect of the teacher's reading aloud on the reading comprehension of EFL students. *ELT Journal, 51*, 43–47.

Asher, J. (1972). Children's first language as a model for second language learning. *Modern Language Journal, 56*, 133–139.

Atkinson, R. C., & Shiffrin, R. M. (1971). The control of short-term memory. *Scientific American, 224*, 82–89.

Baddeley, A. D. (1986). *Working memory*. Oxford: Clarendon Press.

Baddeley, A. D. (2000). The episodic buffer: A new component of working memory? *Trends in Cognitive Sciences, 4*, 417–423.

Baddeley, A. D., Gathercole, S. E., & Papagno, C. (1998). The phonological loop as a language learning device. *Psychological Review, 105*, 158–173.

Baddeley, A. D., & Hitch, G. J. (1974). Working memory. In G. A. Bower (Ed.), *Recent advances in leaning and motivation, Vol. 8* (pp. 47–89). New York: Academic Press.

Baddeley, A. D., Lewis, V., & Vallar, G. (1984). Exploring the articulatory loop. *Quarterly Journal of Experimental Psychology, 36*, 232–252.

Baddeley, A. D., & Logie, R. H. (1999). Working memory: The multiple-component model. In A. Miyake & P. Shah (Eds.), *Models of working memory* (pp. 28–61). New York: Cambridge University Press.

Baddeley, A. D., Thomson, N., & Buchanan, M. (1975). Word length and the structure of short-term memory. *Journal of Verbal Learning and Verbal Behavior, 14*, 575–589.

Ban, H. (2004). Hatsuon gakushu ni okeru gurupu monitaringu katsudo no kanosei — gakushusha no ishiki no henka wo chushin ni — [On the potential of group monitoring during pronunciation practice: Focusing on changes in the learner's consciousness]. *Gengobunka to nihongo kyoiku, 27*, 129–143.

Bartlett, F. C. (1932). *Remembering*. Cambridge: Cambridge University Press.

Bransford, J. D., & Johnson, M. K. (1972). Contextual prerequisites for understanding: Some investigations of comprehension and recall. *Journal of Verbal Learning and Verbal Behavior, 11*, 717–726.

Brown, H. D. (2006). *Teaching by principles: An interactive approach to language pedagogy*. New York: Pearson Longman.

Call, M. E. (1985). Auditory short-term memory, listening comprehension, and the input hypothesis. *TESOL Quarterly, 19*, 765–781.

Carey, P. (1971). Verbal retention after shadowing and after listening. *Perception and Psychophysics, 9*, 79–83.

Carrell, P. (1983). Three components of background knowledge in reading comprehension. *Language Learning, 33*, 183–207.

Chamot, A. U., & Kupper, L. (1989). Learning strategies in foreign language instruction. *Foreign Language Annals, 22*, 13–24.

Collins, A. M., & Loftus, E. F. (1975). A spreading-activation theory of semantic processing. *Psychological Review, 82*, 407–428.

Conrad, R., & Hull, A. J. (1964). Acoustic confusion in immediate memory. *British Journal of Psychology, 55*, 429–432.

Craik, F. M., & Lockhart, R. S. (1972). Level of processing: A framework for memory research. *Journal of Verbal Learning and Verbal Behavior, 11*, 671–684.

Educational Testing Service. (2008). *TOEIC test new official book, Vol. 3*. Tokyo: TOEIC Organization Committee.

Favreau, M., & Segalowitz, N. (1983). Automatic and controlled processes in the first and second-language reading of fluent bilinguals. *Memory

& *Cognition, 11*, 565–574.
Field, J. (2003). Promoting perception: Lexical segmentation in L2 listening. *ELT Journal, 57*, 325–334.
Fries, C. C. (1945). *Teaching and learning English as a foreign language.* Ann Arbor: University of Michigan Press.
Gerver, D. (1974). Simultaneous listening and speaking and retention of prose. *Quarterly Journal of Experimental Psychology, 26*, 337–341.
Ginther, A. (2002). Context and content visuals and performance on listening comprehension stimuli. *Language Testing, 19*, 133–167.
Goodman, K. S. (1967). Reading: A psycholinguistic guessing game. *Literacy Research and Instruction, 6*(4), 126–135.
Herron, C., York, H., Cole, S. P., & Linden, P. (1998). A comparison study of student retention of foreign language video: Declarative versus interrogative advance organizer. *The Modern Language Journal, 82*, 237–247.
Hirai, A. (1999). The relationship between listening and reading rates of Japanese L2 learners. *The Modern Language Journal, 83*, 367–382.
Hyde, T. S., & Jenkins, J. J. (1969). Differential effects of incidental tasks on the organization of recall of lists of highly associated words. *Journal of Experimental Psychology, 82*, 472–481.
Iwashita, M. (2008). Nihongo gakushusha ni okeru shadoingu kunren no yukosei—1kagetsukan no judanteki chosa ni yoru kento— [The efectiveness of shadowing training on Japanese learners—Based on a month-long longtitudinal study—]. *Hiroshima Daigaku Daigakuin Kyouikugaku Kenkyuka Kiyo Dai Nibu, 57*, 219–228.
Jones, L., & Plass, J. (2002). Supporting listening comprehension and vocabulary acquisition in French with multimedia annotations. *The Modern Language Journal, 86*, 546–561.
Kadota, S. (2007). Shadoingu to ondoku no kagaku [Science of shadowing and oral reading].Tokyo: Cosmopier.
Karasawa, M. (2009). Shadoingu ga nihongo gakushusha ni motarasu eikyo: Tanki renshu ni yoru hatsuonmen oyobi gakushusha ishiki no kanten kara [The effect of shadowing exercises on JSL learners' pronunciation

and motivation]. *Ochanomizu Joshi Daigaku Jinbun Kagaku Kenkyu, 6*, 209–220.

Kawabe, S., & Kobashi, Y. (2010). *Daily oral communication I.* Tokyo: Ikeda shoten.

Kikuchi, K., & Nakayama, K. (2006). Gaikoku eiga no risuningu ga chugakusei no gakushu iyoku ni oyobosu eikyo [Listening to English movies: Effects on junior high school students' intrinsic interest in learning English]. *Japanese Journal of Educational Psychology, 54*, 254–264.

Kintsch, W. (1994). Text comprehension, memory, and learning. *American Psychologist, 49*(4), 294–303.

Kintsch, W., Welsch, D., Schmalhofer, F., & Zimny, S. (1990). Sentence memory: A theoretical analysis. *Journal of Memory and Language, 29*, 133–159.

Koike, I. (1993). Eigo no hiaringu to shido [Listening and instruction in English Education]. Tokyo: Taishukan Shoten.

Kurata, K. (2007). Nihongo shadoingu no ninchi mekanizumu ni kansuru kiso kenkyu—koto saisei kaishi jiten, kioku yoryo, bunkozo no shitenkara [A fundamental study on the cognitive mechanism of shadowing in Japanese—from the starting points of oral reproduction, memory span, and sentence structure]. *Hiroshima Daigaku Daigakuin Kyouikugaku Kenkyuka Kiyo Dai Nibu, 56*, 259–265.

Kurata, K. (2008). Nihongo shadoing ni okeru bun no onin imishori ni oyobosu kioku youryo, bun no shurui, bunmyakusei no eikyo—nihongo bogo washa wo taishoto shite [The influence of memory span, sentence type, and context on phonological processing and semantic processing during shadowing in Japanese—a focus on Japanese native speakers]. *Hiroshima Daigaku Daigakuin Kyouikugaku Kenkyuka Kiyo Dai Nibu, 58*, 229–235.

LaBerge, D., & Samuels, S. J. (1974). Toward a theory of automatic information processing in reading. *Cognitive Psychology, 6*, 293–323.

Lado, R. (1950). Survey of tests in English as a foreign language. *Language Learning, 3*, 51–66.

Lambert, S. (1988). Information processing among conference interpreters: A test of the depth-of-processing hypothesis. *Meta: Translators' Journal, 33*, 377–387.

Lambert, S. (2004). Shared attention during sight translation, sight interpretation and simultaneous interpretation. *Meta*, 49, 294–306.

Logie, R. H. (1995). *Visuo-spatial working memory.* Hove: Erlbaum.

Long, D. R. (1989). Listening comprehension: A schema-theoretic perspective. *The Modern Language Journal, 73*, 32–40.

Lynch, T. (1998). Theoretical perspectives on listening. *Annual Review of Applied Linguistics, 18*, 3–19.

Markham, P., Peter, L., & McCarthy, T. (2001). The effects of native language vs. target language captions on foreign language students' DVD video comprehension. *Foreign Language Annals, 34*, 439–445.

McDonough, K., & Trofimovich, P. (2009). *Using priming methods in second language research.* New York: Routledge.

McNamara, D. S., & Kintsch, W. (1996). Learning from texts: Effects of prior knowledge and text coherence. *Discourse Processes, 22*(3), 247–288.

Mendelsohn, D. (1998). Teaching listening. *Annual Review of Applied Linguistics, 18*, 81–101.

Meyer, D. E., & Schvaneveldt, R. W. (1971). Facilitation in recognizing pairs of words: Evidence of a dependence between retrieval operations. *Journal of Experimental Psychology, 90*, 227–234.

Miller, G. A. (1956). The magical number seven, plus minus two: Some limits on our capacity for processing information. *Psychological Review, 63*, 81–97.

Mori, T., & Chujo, K. (2005). Ninchi shinrigaku ki wado [Keywords in cognitive psychology]. Tokyo: Yuhikaku.

Mori, T., Inoue, T., & Matsui, T. (2009). *Gurafic ninchi shinrigaku* [Cognitive psychology]. Tokyo: Saiensu Sha.

Murdock, B. B. (1967). Recent developments in short-term memory. *British Journal of Psychology, 58*, 421–433.

Nakayama, T. (2011a). Bijuaru shadoingu no kouka [The effectiveness of visual shadowing]. *Journal of the Japan Association for Developmental Education, 6*, 151–159.

Nakayama, T. (2011b). Kinogo no hatsuon kyodo no chigai wa shadoingu no gijutsu shincho ni eikyo wo oyobosunoka: Shadoingu wo okonau saino kinogo no jyakkei no kikitori wo sokushin saseru hoho [Weak forms in shadowing: How can Japanese EFL Learners perform better in shadowing tasks?]. *The Studies in English Language, Literature and Culture, 41*, 17–31.

Nakayama, T. (2011c). Memory and language. *Josai University /Josai International University Institute of Inter-Cultural Research, 16*, 77–95.

Nakayama, T., & Armstrong, T. (2015). Weak forms in shadowing: How can Japanese EFL learners perform better on shadowing tasks? *Jissen Women's University CLEIP Journal, 1*, 13–21.

Nakayama, T. & Iwata, A. (2012). Differences in comprehension: Visual stimulus vs. auditory stimulus. *The Language Education Center of Josai University Bulletin, 6*, 1–8.

Nakayama, T., & Mori, T. (2012). Efficacy of visual-auditory shadowing. *The Studies in English Language, Literature and Culture, 42*, 55–68.

Nakayama, T., & Suzuki, A. (2012). Gakushu hourryaku no chigai ga shadoingu no fukushoryo ni ataerueikyo [A study on learning strategies in shadowing training]. *Journal of the Japan Association for Developmental Education, 7,* 131–140.

Nakayama, T., Suzuki, A., & Matsunuma, M. (2015). Shadoinguho wa bunshourikai no dono sokumen ni kouka ga arunoka [Which aspect of listening comprehension does the shadowing method facilitate?]. *Journal of Learning Science, 8*, 203–209.

Neely, J. H. (1977). Semantic priming and retrieval from lexical memory: Roles of inhibitionless spreading activation and limited-capacity attention. *Journal of Experimental Psychology, 106*, 226–254.

Negishi, M., Yoshitomi, A., Kano, A., Shizuka, T., & Takayama, Y. (2007). *Blue oral communication I [revised edition].* Tokyo: Obunsha.

Nomura, K., Ito, M., Oyama, K., Shimamoto, H., Tagaya, S., & Rockenbach, B. (2005). *Voice oral communication I [new edition].*

Tokyo: Daiichi Gakushusha.

Ochi, M. (2005). Koko ni okeru tsuyaku kunrenho wo toriireta gengo kyouiku no kouka to tenbo [The effectiveness and prospect of interpreting training methods of language education in Japanese senior high schools]. *Interpretation Studies, 5*, 203–224.

Oka, N. (2000). Imikioku [Semantic memory]. In N. Ota & H. Taga (Eds.), *Kioku kenkyu no saizensen* (pp. 67–97). Kyoto: Kitaoji Shobo.

O'Malley, M., & Chamot, A. (1990). *Learning strategies in second language acquisition.* New York: Cambridge University Press.

O'Malley, M., Chamot, A., & Kupper, S. (1989). Listening comprehension strategies in second language acquisition. *Applied Linguistics, 10*, 418–437.

Oxford, R. (1993). Research update on teaching L2 listening. *System, 21*, 205–211.

Oyama, Y. (2009). Eibun sokudoku shido ga nihonjin daigakusei no eigo risuningu noryoku no shincho ni ataeru eikyo—dictation kunren tono hikaku [Effect of English text speed reading training on English listening comprehension among Japanese university students—comparison to dictation training]. *Japan Journal of Educational Technology, 32*, 351–358.

Papagno, C., Valentine, T., & Baddeley, A. D. (1991). Phonological short-term memory and foreign language vocabulary learning. *Journal of Memory and Language, 30*, 331–347.

Parkin, A. J. (1984). Levels of processing, context, and facilitation of pronunciation. *Acta Psychologica, 55*, 19–29.

Posner, M. I., & Snyder, C. R. R. (1975). Facilitation and inhibition in the processing of signals. In P. M. A. Rabbitt & S. Dornic (Eds.), *Attention and performance V* (pp. 669–682). New York: Academic Press.

Richards, C. J. (1983). Listening comprehension: Approach, design, procedure. *TESOL Quarterly, 17*, 219–240.

Richards, C. J., & Rodgers, T. (2001). *Approaches and methods in language teaching.* Cambridge: Cambridge University Press.

Rost, M. (2002). *Teaching and researching listening*. New York: Longman.

Rubin, J. (1994). A review of second language listening comprehension research. *Modern Language Journal, 78*, 199–221.

Rumelhart, D. E. (1980). Schemata: The building blocks of cognition. In R. Spiro, B. Bruce, & W. Brewer (Eds.), *Theoretical issues in reading comprehension* (pp. 33–58). New Jersey: Lawrence Erlbaum Associates.

Rumelhart, D. E., Hinton, G. E. & Williams, R. J. (1986). Learning representations by back-propagating errors. *Nature, 323*, 533–536.

Rumelhart, D. E., & Ortony, A. (1977). The representation of knowledge in memory. In R. Spiro & W. Montague (Eds.), *In schooling and the acquisition of knowledge* (pp. 99–135). New Jersey: Lawrence Erlbaum Associates.

Sakoda, K., Furumoto, Y., Nakagami, A., Sakamoto, H., & Goto, M. (2009). Shadoingu jissen ni okeru pea gakushugata tokyoushi shudogata jugyo no hikaku [The analysis of peer and teacher feedback in shadowing practice]. *Hiroshimdaigaku Nihongo Kyoiku Kenkyu, 19*, 31–37.

Santrock, J. W. (1988). *Psychology: The science of mind and behavior*. Dubuque: Wm. G. Brown Publishers.

Sato, T., & Nakamura, N. (1998). Shadowing no koka to gakushushano ishiki [The effects of shadowing and the students' feedback]. *Tsukuba Kokusai Daigaku Kenkyuu Kiyo, 4*, 47–57.

Shiffrin, R., Dumais, S., & Schneider, W. (1981). Characteristics of automatism. In L. Long & A. Baddeley (Eds.), *Attention and performance IX*. New Jersey: Erlbaum.

Shiffrin, R., & Schneider, W. (1977). Controlled and automatic human information processing. Perceptual learning, automatic attending, and a general theory. *Psychological Review, 84*, 127–190.

Shimomura, N., Minematsu, N., Yamauchi, Y., & Hirose, K. (2008). Bottom-up kurasutarinngu woo mochiita shadouing onseino jido hyotei [Automatic scoring of language learners' utterances generated through shadowing based on bottom-up clustering]. *Technical Report of IEICE, 38*, 187–192.

Shirahata, T., Wakabayashi, S., & Muranoi, H. (2010). *Shosetsu daini gengo shutoku kenkyu rironkara kenkyuhomade* [Explication of second language acquisition research: From theory to practice]. Tokyo: Kenkyusha.

Sudo, M. (2010). *Eigo no onsei shutoku no seisei to chikaku no mekanizumu* [Mechanism of generation of phonological learning and perception of English]. Tokyo: Kazama Shobo.

Takefuta, Y. (1984). *Hiaringu no Kodo Kagaku* [Behavioral science in hearing]. Tokyo: Kenkyusha.

Takizawa, S. (2002). Gogaku kyouka ho toshiteno tsuyaku kunren ho to sono oyo rei. [Interpreter training techniques and their application as a tool for language enhancement]. *Bulletin of Hokuriku University, 26*, 63–72.

Tamai, K. (1992). "Follow-up" no chokairyoku kojo ni oyobosu koka oyobi "follow-up" noryoku to chokairyoku no kankei. Dai 4 kai "Eiken" kenkyu josei hokoku [The effect of follow-up on listening comprehension]. *STEP Bulletin, 4*, 48–62.

Tamai, K. (1997). Shadowing no koka to chokai process ni okeru ichizuke. [The effectiveness of shadowing and its position in the listening process]. *Current English Studies, 36*, 105–116.

Tamai, K. (2005). *Risuningu shidoho to shiteno shadoingu no koka ni kansuru kenkyu* [Research on the effect of shadowing as a listening instruction method]. Tokyo: Kazama Shobo.

Tanaka, M. (2004). Tsuyaku kuren ho wo riyoushita daigaku deno eigo kyouiku no jissai to mondaiten [Current pedagogical issues in teaching interpreting at the undergraduate level]. *Interpretation Studies, 5*, 63–82.

Trofimovich, P., & McDonough, K. (2011). *Applying priming methods to L2 learning, teaching and research*. Philadelphia: John Benjamins Publishing Co.

Tsui, A. B. M., & Fullilove, J. (1998). Bottom-up or top-down processing as a discriminator of L2 listening performance. *Applied Liniguistics, 19*, 432–451.

Tulving, E. (1972). *Episodic and semantic memory*. In E. Tulving & W.

Donaldson (Eds.), *Organization of memory* (pp. 381–402). New York: Academic Press.

Tweedy, J. R., Lapinsky, R. H., & Schvaneveldt, R. W. (1977). Semantic-context effects on word recognition: Influence of varying the proportion of items presented in an appropriate context. *Memory & Cognition, 5*(1), 84–89.

Vandergrift, L. (2004). Listening to learn or learning to listen. *Annual Review of Applied Linguistics, 24*, 3–25.

van Dijk, T. A., & Kintsch, W. (1983). *Strategies of discourse comprehension.* New York: Academic Press.

Wilding, J. (1986). Joint effects of semantic priming and repetition in a lexical decision task: Implications for a model of lexical access. *Quarterly Journal of Experimental Psychology, 38*, 213–228.

Yanagihara, Y. (1995). Eigo chokairyoku no shidoho ni kansuru jikkenteki kenkyu—shadouingu to deikuteshon no kokani tsuite [A study of teaching methods for developing English listening comprehension—the effects of shadowing and dictation]. *Language Laboratory, 32*, 73–89.

Yata, Y., Kohashi, Y., Tamura, H., & Nishimiya, T. (2010). *Why not? Oral Communication I.* Tokyo: Ikeda Shoten.

Index

Author Index

A
Amer 92
Asher 13
Atkinson 3, 21
B
Baddeley 3, 20, 21, 22, 31, 32, 33, 34, 35, 36, 37, 92
Ban 25
Bartlett 12
Bransford 30
Brown, H. D. 35
C
Call 9
Carey 24
Carrell 3
Chamot 9, 13, 14, 24, 25
Chamot 9, 13, 14, 24, 25

Chujo 32
Cole 13
Colins 40
Conrad 34
Craik 3
D
Dumais 5
F
Favreau 5, 6, 9,
Field 5, 8, 9, 42, 65
Fries 11
Fullilove 3, 14
Furumoto 19
G
Gerver
Gnther 23, 24
Goodman 3, 13

Goto 19
H
Herron 13
Hirose 61
Hull 34
Hyde 3
I
Inoue 39
Iwashita 19, 24, 35, 37
Iwata 5, 36, 42, 65,
J
Jenkins 3
Johnson 30
Jones 13
K
Kadota 4, 9, 18, 19, 21, 22, 37, 42
Kano 49
Karasawa 19, 37
Kawabe 49
Kikuchi 63
Kintsch 4, 30, 31, 44, 46, 87, 92
Kohashi 49
Koike 7, 9, 26, 42, 65
Kupper 9, 13, 14, 24, 26
Kupper 9, 13, 14, 24, 25
Kurata 22, 24
L
LaBerge 21
Lado 11
Lambert 15, 17, 23, 24
Lapinsky 6
Linden 13
Lockhart 3
Loftus 40

Logie 3, 21, 35
Long 3
Lynch 13
M
Markham 13
Matsui 39
McCarthy 13
McDonough 38, 40, 41, 43
McNamara 30
Mendelsohn 13
Meyer 6, 39
Miller 3, 32
Minematsu 61
Mori 32, 39
Muranoi 15
Murdock 3
N
Nakagami 19
Nakamura 19, 22
Nakayama, K. 63
Nakayama, T. 5, 22, 25, 26, 27, 36, 42, 45, 46, 47, 57, 60, 52, 63, 65, 69, 80
Neely 6, 7
Negishi 49
Nishimiya 49
Nomura 49
O
Ochi 23, 42
Oka 39, 40
O'Malley 9, 13, 14, 24
Oxford 13
Oyama, Y. 15, 35, 36, 37

P

Papagno 20, 31
Parkin 3
Peter 13
Plass 13
Posner 6, 21, 39, 40

R

Richards 9, 12, 14, 29
Rodgers 12
Rost 13
Rubin 13, 14
Rumelhart 12, 13

S

Sakamoto 19
Sakoda 19
Samuels 21
Santrock 3
Sato 19, 22
Schneider 5, 21
Schvaneveldt 6
Schvaneveldt 6
Segalowitz 5, 6, 10
Shiffrin 3, 21
Shiffrin 3, 5, 21
Shimomura, N. 61, 62
Shirahata 15
Shizuka 49
Snyder 6, 21, 39, 40

Sudo 7, 9, 42, 65,
Suzuki 25, 26, 27, 45, 46, 57, 60, 62, 69, 80

T

Takefuta 68
Takizawa 15
Tamai 9, 15, 17, 18, 19, 20, 21, 22, 23, 29, 35, 37, 42, 61, 87
Tamura 49
Tanaka, M. 23, 42
Trofimovich 38
Tsui 3, 14, 39,
Tulving 33
Tweedy 6

V

Valentine 20
van Dijk 30, 31, 92
Vandergrift 11, 13, 29

W

Wakabayashi 15
Wilding 29

Y

Yamauchi 61
Yanagihara 15, 17, 19, 23, 37
Yata 49
York 13
Yoshitomi 49

Subject Index

A
assimilaton 8
attentional resources 10, 14, 22, 25, 87, 93
audio-lingual approach 11, 12
auditory input 2-5, 8-9, 18-22, 24, 26, 31-38, 41-43, 57, 58, 65-67, 72, 73, 76, 77, 86, 87, 92, 93
automatic 5, 6, 40, 43

B
background knowledge 12, 13
Behaviorism 11
bottom-up processing 5, 13, 14

C
cliticization 8
cognitive psychology 12, 13, 29, 31, 40
commonalities 2, 33
connected speech 8,
content word 26, 59, 63-65, 71, 72, 75, 76
contrastive analysis 11
controlled 5, 6, 40, 43

D
dictation 14, 15, 20, 36, 49, 52

E
elision 8
encoding 3, 31, 33, 37
ESL 8
expectancy 6, 7

F
function word 26, 42, 59, 62-65, 71, 72, 75, 76, 91

I
Interactive Activation Model 13

L
L1 2, 5, 11, 24, 29, 43
language processing 2, 5, 9, 31, 44, 92
learning transfer 30

M
magnitude 6
metanl representation 4, 30
modality 4, 36, 43
mora 7, 8
multicomponent model 32
mumbling 18, 19

N
non-word 7

O
off-line 4, 9, 66
on-line 4, 9, 24, 25, 35, 36, 65, 66

P
pair-work 25
parallel reading 18
parsing 29
perception 17, 24
phonetic variations 8, 22, 87, 93
phonological coding 20-22, 26, 27, 35-39, 56, 87, 90, 93
phonological loop 22, 32-35, 42

Post Method Era   13, 14
prime-target word pair   6
priming   6, 38-44, 57, 89
priming effect   6, 38, 39-44
prior knowledge   3, 23, 30
propositional textbase   4, 84
prosody shadowing   18
psycholinguistics   12

R

reading aloud   17-19, 26, 27, 35-38, 41, 43, 44, 51, 56-58, 65, 66, 72, 77, 90-93
reinforcement   11
resyllabification   8
retention   3, 21, 27, 31, 33, 35
retrieval   3, 21, 27, 33, 35
rhythmic structures   7, 8, 26

S

schema   12, 13
selective attention   17
self-monitoring   23-27, 45, 55, 57
self-monitoring strategy   24, 25
semantic memory   7, 40
semantic priming   6, 39

seonsory register   32
shadowing   15, 17, 18-20, 23-27, 30, 31, 35, 37, 38, 41, 42-47, 49, 51-93
sight-translation   15
situation model   4, 30-31, 44, 46-48, 50, 53-56, 81, 83-87, 93
stress-timed   8
structural linguistics   11
surface structure   4, 30, 48, 53-55, 84, 85
syllable   8, 61, 62

T

target   6, 7, 38, 39, 40, 41, 62
top-down processing   2, 3, 12-14

U

utilization   29

V

visual-auditory shadowing   72, 73, 77, 79, 82, 85-87, 91-93

W

word recognition   5-9
working memory   3, 4, 9, 20, 21, 27, 32, 33, 42

Introduction of Author

NAKAYAMA, Tomokazu is an Associate Professor at the Center for Language Education and International Programs at Jissen Women's University in Tokyo. He teaches not only English but also teacher training courses. He received an MA in TESOL from Columbia Teachers' College in 2005 and a Ph.D in Education from Hiroshima University in 2013. He has also taught at Josai University in Saitama, Obirin Junior & Senior High School in Tokyo and Suiryo Junior & Senior High School in Yokohama. His recent paper was accepted in the Journal of English as an International Language. He is also a co-author of an English textbook titled *hyaku topikkku de manabu jissen eigo toreiningu* (Practical English Training through 100 Topics). His main research interests are VA shadowing, listening instructions, English as an International Language, and oral proficiency.

Efficacy of Visual-Auditory Shadowing Method
in SLA Based on Language Processing Models
in Cognitive Psychology

著　者	中 山 誠 一	
発行者	武 村 哲 司	
印刷所	日之出印刷株式会社	

2017 年 1 月 27 日　　第 1 版第 1 刷発行Ⓒ
2017 年 2 月 7 日　　　　第 2 刷発行

発行所　株式会社　開 拓 社　　〒113-0023 東京都文京区向丘 1-5-2
　　　　　　　　　　　　　　　　電話　(03) 5842-8900 (代表)
　　　　　　　　　　　　　　　　振替　00160-8-39587
　　　　　　　　　　　　　　　　http://www.kaitakusha.co.jp

ISBN978-4-7589-2236-4　C3082

JCOPY ＜(社)出版者著作権管理機構 委託出版物＞

本書の無断複写は，著作権法上での例外を除き禁じられています．複写される場合は，そのつど事前に，(社)出版者著作権管理機構 (電話 03-3513-6969, FAX 03-3513-6979, e-mail: info@jcopy.or.jp) の許諾を得てください．